THE COMPLETE IDIOT'S GUIDE® TO

Campus Safety

by Guy J. Antinozzi, J.D., and Alan Axelrod, Ph.D.

ALPHA

A member of Penguin Group (USA) Inc.

ALPHA BOOKS

Published by the Penguin Group

Penguin Group (USA) Inc., 375 Hudson Street, New York, New York 10014, USA

Penguin Group (Canada), 90 Eglinton Avenue East, Suite 700, Toronto, Ontario M4P 2Y3, Canada (a division of Pearson Penguin Canada Inc.)

Penguin Books Ltd., 80 Strand, London WC2R 0RL, England

Penguin Ireland, 25 St. Stephen's Green, Dublin 2, Ireland (a division of Penguin Books Ltd.)

Penguin Group (Australia), 250 Camberwell Road, Camberwell, Victoria 3124, Australia (a division of Pearson Australia Group Pty. Ltd.)

Penguin Books India Pvt. Ltd., 11 Community Centre, Panchsheel Park, New Delhi—110 017, India

Penguin Group (NZ), 67 Apollo Drive, Rosedale, North Shore, Auckland 1311, New Zealand (a division of Pearson New Zealand Ltd.)

Penguin Books (South Africa) (Pty.) Ltd., 24 Sturdee Avenue, Rosebank, Johannesburg 2196, South Africa

Penguin Books Ltd., Registered Offices: 80 Strand, London WC2R 0RL, England

International Standard Book Number: 978-1-59257-743-9
Library of Congress Catalog Card Number: 2007939747

10   09   08   8   7   6   5   4   3   2   1

Interpretation of the printing code: The rightmost number of the first series of numbers is the year of the book's printing; the rightmost number of the second series of numbers is the number of the book's printing. For example, a printing code of 08-1 shows that the first printing occurred in 2008.

Printed in the United States of America

Note: This publication contains the opinions and ideas of its authors. It is intended to provide helpful and informative material on the subject matter covered. It is sold with the understanding that the authors and publisher are not engaged in rendering professional services in the book. If the reader requires personal assistance or advice, a competent professional should be consulted.

The authors and publisher specifically disclaim any responsibility for any liability, loss, or risk, personal or otherwise, which is incurred as a consequence, directly or indirectly, of the use and application of any of the contents of this book.

Most Alpha books are available at special quantity discounts for bulk purchases for sales promotions, premiums, fund-raising, or educational use. Special books, or book excerpts, can also be created to fit specific needs.

For details, write: Special Markets, Alpha Books, 375 Hudson Street, New York, NY 10014.

Publisher: *Marie Butler-Knight*
Editorial Director: *Mike Sanders*
Senior Managing Editor: *Billy Fields*
Executive Editor: *Randy Ladenheim-Gil*
Development Editor: *Lynn Northrup*
Senior Production Editor: *Janette Lynn*

Copy Editor: *Amy Borrelli*
Cover Designer: *Bill Thomas*
Book Designer: *Trina Wurst*
Indexer: *Heather McNeill*
Layout: *Brian Massey*
Proofreader: *John Etchison*

To Anita and Ian
—AA
To Jennifer, Joshua, Salvatore, Vincent, Vito, Dominic, Luca, Anthony, Mia, and Rudy.
—GA

Contents at a Glance

Contents

Introduction

On April 16, 2007, 23-year-old Seung Hui Cho opened fire with semi-automatic weapons on fellow students at Virginia Tech, in Blacksburg, Virginia, killing 32, wounding 21, then killing himself.

Virginia Tech President Charles Steger announced: "Today the university was struck with a tragedy that we consider of monumental proportions. The university is shocked and indeed horrified."

What else could he say? What else could he feel other than shock and horror?

More than 5,000 years of recorded history have accustomed us to accept violent death in war. Newspapers and television have long shown us that the streets of America's cities can be dangerous, even bloody places. Since at least September 11, 2001, we have been made aware of the potential for terrorist mayhem every time we pass through metal detectors and other checkpoints as we prepare to board a commercial airliner.

But a college campus?

A college campus is supposed to be a place of learning, of free inquiry, of intellectual challenge, of preparation for a career, of personal growth. It's supposed to be a stimulating, even a joyous place, and certainly secure—a haven for the mind and imagination.

Hence the shock and horror. Violence on campus. Who expects it?

In fact, the lockdown of Virginia Tech after the shootings was the *second* time in less than a year that a shooting had closed the campus. In August 2006, the opening day of classes had to be postponed when an escaped prison inmate allegedly gunned down a hospital guard, then fled to the Virginia Tech area. Just off campus, the inmate shot and killed a sheriff's deputy before he was, at last, apprehended.

Mass murder is a rare event on campus, but crime, violent as well as nonviolent, is as common in the college and university community as anywhere else in American society. Nor is the campus immune from other kinds of violence, such as fire and accident. College students can suffer injury, illness, and life-threatening emotional crises just as anyone anywhere else can.

On balance, college life probably presents no more risks than life outside of the campus. There is, however, one risk unique to the college and university: the risk that we will fail to understand that, while the campus is no more dangerous than anywhere else, it is no safer, either. If there are no more risks inside the college community than outside of it, there certainly are no fewer.

How to Use This Book

Denial of risk is the greatest hazard of life in the campus community. The purpose of this book is not to paint college in lurid hues of blood, but to identify the risks, the hazards, as well as the outright dangers, and—most important—to present strategies for avoiding or minimizing them and, if necessary, for surviving them.

Knowledge is power. That is the foundation on which any college or university is built. That is also the underlying assumption of this book. It's organized into four parts:

Part 1, "First Things First," helps you to hone your people skills in order to enhance your personal security. This part also gives you the information you need to help you select a safe and secure school and to help you evaluate the security situation at the college or university you currently attend.

Part 2, "On Campus and Off," covers living safely and with a minimum of stress on campus. Chapters are devoted to residence hall living; to the Greek experience of sorority and fraternity living; to keeping your personal property secure; and to using Internet resources safely, including everything from defending your personal data and securing your identity to controlling the risks of social websites, online dating, and Internet merchant sites. You will also find a chapter on staying safe off campus, whether you are driving your car, using public transportation, or taking to your own two feet. Finally, this part includes a chapter devoted to alcohol and drugs and a special chapter on spring break.

Part 3, "The People You Meet," focuses on relationships: with your roommate or roommates, in dating scenarios, and where strangers are concerned—especially disturbing and possibly dangerous strangers.

Part 4, "Getting Help and Helping Yourself," offers a chapter on identifying and coping with health emergencies, stress, and emotional crises. You'll also find advice on who to turn to for help with academic questions, matters of financial aid, issues of health, psychological counseling, and spiritual guidance. Included as well is everything you need to know about working with your campus police force. The final chapter is all about physically defending your life—how to avoid trouble and what to do if trouble finds you nevertheless.

At the very end of this book is a quick-reference list of common emergencies and what to do about each of them.

Extras

In addition to the main narrative of *The Complete Idiot's Guide to Campus Safety*, you'll find other types of useful information, including safety tips; things, actions, and behavior to avoid; relevant stats and quick facts; and websites, articles, books, and other resources to help you stay safe on campus and off. Look for these sidebars:

Bad Idea!

Here you'll find some of the most common poor choices students (and others) make—and how not to make them yourself.

Little Black Book

Look here for advice on websites and other sources of information to alert you to hazards and enable you to cope with them.

Safe Move

This feature passes along tips to enhance your security.

Hard Fact

This feature supplies stats and facts that will help you stay safe.

Acknowledgments

My thanks and respect to my co-author, Guy Antinozzi, law enforcement officer, consultant, and expert.

As always, I am grateful for the fine work and support of the folks at Alpha Books, especially Randy Ladenheim-Gil and Lynn Northrup.

> —Alan Axelrod

I would like to thank my wife, Jennifer. Her intelligence, kindness, love, and support make possible all of my achievements. She is my not-so-secret source of wisdom and guidance. My son Salvatore is deployed with the U.S. Army in Iraq, and my son Joshua serves as a firefighter in Cobb County, Georgia. They have my gratitude for their service and the sense of pride they give me daily.

Matt Kelly and Frank Beard of HRH provided me with the opportunity to utilize my skills in a wonderfully supportive setting. The people of HRH prove daily that business can be conducted effectively while maintaining the highest ethical standards. Chief Rus Drew continues to set the standard in campus law enforcement. Karen Newman is a fine grandmother to our sons and always supportive of my success. I am forever grateful to her. My co-author, Alan Axelrod, is fun to work with and very talented. Without him, I would still be hoping to someday write a book.

Finally, the men and women of campus law enforcement deserve our thanks and acknowledgment. Their dedication to this highly specialized and demanding aspect of public safety usually goes unrecognized. But their effect on the well-being of students is immeasurable.

> —Guy Antinozzi

Trademarks

All terms mentioned in this book that are known to be or are suspected of being trademarks or service marks have been appropriately capitalized. Alpha Books and Penguin Group (USA) Inc. cannot attest to the accuracy of this information. Use of a term in this book should not be regarded as affecting the validity of any trademark or service mark.

Part 1

First Things First

The first chapter in this part helps you to prepare for a safe and secure college experience by giving you tips on honing your "people reading" skills, which will help you stay out of trouble and, if necessary, get out of trouble. The second chapter is all about assessing the crime and safety picture at the schools you are considering enrolling in as well as at the school you finally choose.

Chapter 1

Making It on Your Own

In This Chapter

- ◆ What to watch out for
- ◆ Scammers and predators
- ◆ Staying safe in crowded places
- ◆ Practicing "relaxed awareness"
- ◆ Using and "reading" body language
- ◆ How to spot the bad guys

You are a college student. What does that mean, exactly?

You are probably pretty smart, maybe very smart. You have at least enough curiosity to explore new ideas and new directions in your life. You are either looking for a career, or you already have a career in mind. Either way, you are probably success oriented and goal directed.

What else?

You are excited about being away from home and parents for the first time in your life. You are also a little scared by this new independence. Maybe more than a little. On the other hand, chances are that you're not entirely independent. If you're like most undergrads, you still rely—at least partially—on your parents for financial support. Even so, Mom and Dad aren't breathing down your neck every day. Nor are they there to look after you every day.

Whatever else you learn in college, you learn a lot about yourself. You learn about who you are, as you get your first extended experience of independence—or at least semi-independence—and study and live with a growing awareness that you are moving toward the greater degree of independence graduation day will bring.

Great Expectations

Different people expect college to be different things. Some look forward to learning, the opening up of new worlds of knowledge, the preparation for a career. Some are eager for an expanded social life. Some are eager for the intellectual and social challenges that await them, while others are apprehensive about these.

The one expectation no one has is that they will become a victim of a crime or an accident.

Now, it can be argued that very few of us—in college, out of college, wherever—go around in the expectation of imminent misfortune. But the fact is that most students go off to college not only feeling that they will be protected, but that the campus itself is somehow a world apart from the "real world," a kind of cocoon nothing bad can penetrate.

The events of April 16, 2007, at Virginia Tech, a pleasant campus in a good community noted for its safety, shattered this illusion—horrifically. Armed with a pair of semiautomatic handguns, a deranged student went on a murderous rampage, ending the lives of 32 and wounding 25 others before committing suicide.

> **Hard Fact**
>
> According to the National Safety Council, the odds that you will die in an accident in any one year are 1 in 1,743. Lifetime odds are 1 in 22. The odds of being killed in a criminal assault are 1 in 16,402 for any year, and 1 in 211 lifetime.

The shooter was a VT undergraduate, 23-year-old Seung-Hui Cho, a South Korean citizen and permanent U.S. resident. He was described as "a loner" and had been investigated by the university police for stalking and harassing two female students. Signs of mental illness were clear. Not only did more than one VT professor report that his writing was "disturbing," he had been declared mentally ill by a Virginia special justice in 2005 and ordered to seek outpatient treatment. Two days after the rampage, on April 18, 2007, NBC News received a package from Cho containing a rambling 1,800-word manifesto, photos, and 27 digitally recorded videos in which the young man compared himself to Christ and ranted against the wealthy.

We search in vain to derive any good from this spasm of insanity, but it does drive home a key lesson: not that we should fear a nightmare of terrorism at school, but that a college campus is by no means immune to all the bad things that can happen to anyone anywhere else. Crime—ranging from the horrific to the minor and annoying—and catastrophe stalk the campus and the college town just as they do the big city and the rural lane.

Criminal Curriculum

In 1986, after a young woman was murdered on the campus of the college she attended, her parents successfully lobbied to gain passage of federal legislation requiring colleges and universities to compile and disclose annual statistics on student-related crime. As we will see in Chapter 2, the Jeanne Clery Disclosure of Campus Policy and Campus Crime Statistics Act, passed in 1990 and better known more simply as the Clery Act, provides students and parents an objective measure by which to gauge the security of their current campus or—even more usefully—a *prospective* institution.

> **Little Black Book**
>
> You can read more about the Clery Act at www.securityoncampus.org/schools/cleryact. All colleges and universities must comply with the act by making timely crime statistics available to the public. Many institutions make these accessible on their websites.

The statistics published pursuant to the Clery Act reveal that colleges and universities are hardly immune to the crimes that afflict society at large and that there is nothing special about most campus crime. It tends to fall into the same seven major categories of crime in the world beyond the campus: homicide, sex offenses, robbery, assault, burglary, grand theft auto, and arson. Some categories of crime are more directly related to college life. These include hazing—usually related to fraternity and even sorority initiation rituals—abuse of alcohol (especially binge drinking) and drugs, specifically targeted scams, and the sexual exploitation of students by other students.

We will discuss hazing and substance abuse in Chapters 4 and 8, and scams and exploitation in Chapters 4 and 6, but those latter two categories deserve a preview here.

Most college students are not financially independent. The apron strings may be cut, but the family purse strings are usually still firmly attached. Nevertheless, living away from home for much of the year, many young people are managing their money for the first time without daily parental supervision. The world has always been plentifully stocked with people who (in the words of master nineteenth-century showman P. T. Barnum) are adept at "separating ladies and gentlemen from their coin." The less experienced the victim, the easier the target, and since college students are typically inexperienced in the management of finances, they make inviting targets for swindlers, thieves, and scammers of all kinds—especially those who operate on the Internet. Scams are not unique to campuses, of course, but for would-be crooks, colleges and universities offer choice pickings.

Bad Idea!

You get an unsolicited e-mail offering a great credit card with virtually no spending limit and an APR way below prime. All you need to do is click and furnish every bit of personal identification information you have. The e-mail even links to a website that looks like that of a major financial institution. Should you click and apply? Bad idea! "Phishing" scams—attempts to get personal and financial information for the purpose of identity theft—are among the most common Internet crimes. You've heard of the gift that keeps on giving? Identity theft is the crime that keeps on taking. A few phone calls are rarely sufficient to clear it up. You may be plagued for months or even years, and you may find it very difficult to get credit.

Sexual exploitation, discussed further in Chapters 4, 6, and 11, is another crime hardly peculiar to the campus, yet one to which some aspects of college life are especially conducive. Violent rape can occur anywhere, of course, but many violent sexual offenders regard the campus as their personal hunting ground, a place amply stocked with young women. Similarly, so-called date rape or acquaintance rape—nonconsensual sexual activity between people who are known to each other, whether platonically or sexually—is all too common outside of the campus, but because of the social nature of co-ed college life, it may occur even more frequently in the college or university setting.

Often, date rape and other forms of sexual exploitation are associated with drinking and, less frequently, with so-called "date-rape drugs" (the most common being Rohypnol, known by a variety of street names, including "roofies"). On a number of college campuses in recent years, sexual exploitation under intoxication has also come to include being photographed in the nude or in sexually explicit and compromising situations. A young woman may awake one morning—or afternoon—with a bad hangover, recalling little or nothing of the night before, and then discover that she is on display on a pornographic university website and/or the Internet at large. It can happen. It does happen. And it may happen—in college.

Safety in Numbers?

Of the innumerable well-worn sayings that guide our lives, one of the most thoroughly worn is this: "There is safety in numbers."

To some extent, this old saying is reliably true. Most of us instinctively avoid deserted city streets at night, but have no qualms about navigating well-traveled routes regardless of the hour. Yet it is also the case that crowded environments present dangers of their own, both in terms of simple safety and crime. Crowds can get out of control. Pushing and shoving—at athletic or entertainment events—can result in injury. Crowded lines, crowded buildings, or even crowded streets are prime ground for pickpockets and purse snatchers, who can, in crowds, get closer to you than would otherwise be acceptable and whose actions are more likely to go unnoticed when you are already getting jostled by others.

Crowds in public places are not the only contradiction of the "safety in numbers" mantra. College is more or less "crowded" all of the time. Dormitory buildings may be bustling. Classrooms and other spaces have a lot of coming and going. There is plenty of distraction, and it is not always possible to distinguish between who legitimately belongs in a dorm or a classroom and who does not. No wonder certain items of personal property—a laptop computer, a costly graphing calculator, an iPod, a purse, a briefcase, a backpack—suddenly "walk off" or "disappear."

Robbery and burglary are hardly crimes peculiar to the college campus, but the campus is a place where thieves can expect to find a good deal of high-value, highly portable property, as well as an environment buzzing with activity—and therefore distraction—yet also an environment that tends to lull prospective victims into feeling at ease and off guard.

Develop Relaxed Attention

The wonderful thing about college is that it is a community full of excitement of all kinds—intellectual and physical—a very public place, yet one in which we feel comfortable, relaxed, safe, and secure. The campus offers much of the stimulation of an exciting downtown urban environment, yet we typically feel none of the threat—none of the reason for wariness—that we sense in many urban places.

These good college feelings do have a downside. We may get so comfortable, so relaxed, that our feeling of safety and security blinds us to real dangers. Whatever else a victim may be—whether a victim of accident or crime—he or she is typically unaware, unwary, and nonvigilant. Most of the time, accident and crime are sneak attacks. We don't expect them. We aren't ready for them. We don't know enough to avoid them.

Does this mean that part of being a college student is to walk about campus anticipating a terrible accident or expecting to be mugged?

Not at all. Even if it could somehow make you safer—which it cannot do—chronic anxiety is no way to live. The best way to stay safe is to see yourself as neither invulnerable nor a target, but as a person with sufficient savvy and vigilance to avoid becoming a victim. The best approach to campus life in general is the approach that the most successful students take to the time they spend in the classroom. It is an attitude of relaxed attention: eyes and mind open, full awareness of what's going on and being said and done around you, and freedom from the potentially self-destructive illusion that nothing bad can happen in the campus cocoon.

College life, as we've already pointed out, presents both the safety and the dangers of numbers—of crowds—but, ultimately, the greatest risk is not being distracted *by others* but becoming *self-absorbed.* The word that is most frequently used is *preoccupied.* It is a very descriptive word. For if you are *pre*occupied, your mind and your senses have been *pre*empted and therefore are unavailable in the present, the here and now—the very space and time in which bad things can happen.

> **Safe Move**
>
> Staying alert and being observant not only enhance your enjoyment of life—in college and out—but are essential to survival. Crime and accidents can happen to anyone at any time, but the most likely victims are the distracted and the preoccupied. Acquire an attitude of relaxed awareness.

Perhaps you are thinking about a calculus problem when you should be watching how you walk down the stairs. Maybe you're on your cell phone when you should be concentrating on driving. Maybe you are so worried about getting to class on time that you don't watch for traffic as you cross the street. Perhaps you've been staring at your laptop screen so long that you don't notice that it's two o'clock in the morning and where you're sitting in the student union is completely deserted—and pretty scary.

Relaxed awareness is not about being anxious. It's about living in the moment, about shedding *pre*occupations so that you can be occupied with the people, the objects, and the possibilities of the *here* and *now.*

How to Be a People Person

We all have our own personal styles, our ways of relating to others. Some new college students devote a great deal of thought to the image they want to project, working hard to come on friendly or maybe to come on aloof and above it all. Others just act as they always have—and that may range from outgoing to loner.

Whatever your personal style, one of the most productive steps you can take in starting your college career is to decide that you will be a people person. There is a very good reason for this. Whatever your field of interest or your major, you are first and foremost in the people business. Everything you study, everything you do involves people, whether it's persuading a professor that you deserve an A or talking your roommate into lending you a few dollars. Everything in college life is a person-to-person transaction.

This doesn't mean you have to put on a phony superfriendly front, but it does mean that you should open and keep open all lines of communication. Listen to others—what interests *them*, what *they* need, what *they* want. And let others know what interests you, what you need, what you want. Recognize yourself as part of a community, a community your active presence helps to create. In time of need, offer help, and when you need help, ask for it.

Safe Move

A lot of us are reluctant to ask for help, even when we really need it. We believe that we are imposing on others, and that others will resent it. The truth is that most people like being asked to help, and they enjoy being helpful. Asking someone for help is a vote of confidence for that person. It is empowering. Want to make someone feel really good? Ask that person for help.

Announcing Yourself

We announce ourselves every day:

"Hello, I'm John Doe."

Most of the time, we go further:

"Hello, I'm John Doe. I need to register for Calculus 101." (You've now announced yourself as a person who needs to register for a certain class.)

And even further:

"Hello, I'm John Doe. I'm interested in joining the Astronomy Club. I've been an amateur astronomer since the third grade." (You are sharing an interest, a passion.)

It's no secret, of course, that people do a lot of their communicating—in various ways, announcing themselves, letting others know just who they are—through language. One popular definition of *human being* is "the animal that uses language." And yet verbal language—the language of words—is not the only language by which we announce ourselves.

In 1970, a writer named Julius Fast published a runaway bestseller called *Body Language*. In it, he revealed what psychologists as well as successful communicators—master salespeople, powerful orators, great actors, and the like—had long known: much of any message one person delivers to another is nonverbal, a matter not of words, but of gestures and glances.

Just how much? A year after *Body Language* appeared, the American psychologist Albert Merabian published a study in which he concluded that listeners evaluate the "emotional content"—the persuasive power—of a speech mostly on the basis of facial expressions and body movement. He estimated that nonverbal, entirely visual cues accounted for more than half—55 percent—of a given speaker's ability to persuade others. Vocal qualities, such as tone and pitch of voice, represented 38 percent. The actual verbal content of a given speech accounted for a mere 7 percent.

Find this hard to believe? Anyone who takes a course in modern U.S. history reads about the nationally broadcasted debates between John F. Kennedy and Richard M. Nixon during the 1960 presidential campaign. Important as historians consider this debate, it produced at the time no clear winner. That's because most people who listened to the debate on radio thought Nixon was more persuasive, whereas a majority who watched the debates on television judged Kennedy the winner. The TV viewers said that Nixon *looked* nervous. His body language was shifty and evasive, and (unfortunately for him) he sweated visibly and profusely. JFK, in contrast, was suave, cool, and yet intense. Whereas Nixon rarely met the camera "eye to eye," JFK continually made a direct visual connection with his audience.

Learning to make your body language work for you—to announce yourself with confidence—not only helps you establish rapport with those around you, it communicates the kind of strength and awareness rarely associated with people who are targeted by criminals. In other words, it tends to broadcast a "hands-off" message to them.

Making an Entrance

There are certain people who always get noticed when they enter a room. We say that they "really know how to make an entrance."

There's no denying that the entrance you make creates the all-important first impression on those around you. No matter how tall or short you are, walk tall. Tall people tend to command greater authority than short people. Is this shallow and unfair? Sure, but it's the way things are. If you are on the short side, develop a confident stride with impeccable posture. Don't hesitate, and don't cringe, stoop, or slouch.

Lower Your Voice

For most people, a deep voice conveys more authority than a high-pitched one. This applies whether a man or a woman is speaking. Consciously pitching your voice a little lower than what's normal for you lends more authority to what you say and makes you sound more confident. It also tends to slow the tempo of your speech, encouraging the more precise articulation of each word. You won't speed, and you won't mumble.

Also be aware that high-pitched, rapid speech is associated with—and communicates—anxiety. Are you anxious? Deliberately lowering the pitch of your voice will not only disguise your anxiety, it may actually help relieve it.

Frightened Because We Run

Another effective antidote to anxiety is good, productive breathing. Nervousness and apprehension produce shortness of breath, and shortness of breath in turn tends to exacerbate feelings of anxiety. It is the most vicious of vicious circles. Think about your breathing. Focus on it. Don't let it come fast and shallow. Instead, breathe deeply and slowly. Breathe as if you have never felt better—and you may soon find that you do, in fact, feel better.

The late nineteenth- and early twentieth-century American philosopher-psychologist William James observed that we do not run because we are frightened, we are frightened because we run. Much of the anxiety you may feel as you go about your day comes from awareness of the unpleasant feelings associated with anxiety itself. The faster your heart beats, the tenser your muscles, the more you feel anxious; and the more anxious you are, the faster your heart beats, the tenser your muscles become, and the more your butterflies beget butterflies. Effective breathing can help break this anxiety cycle and put you in position to project quiet confidence.

A Body Language Glossary

Communicating—nonverbally—an image of relaxed awareness, of energy in confident repose, not only helps you to relate more effectively to everyone around you, it also sends a powerful message to those who might be out to victimize you: *pick another target.* Consider what follows as a basic body language glossary:

◆ Avoid projecting "nervous energy" with rapid-fire speech, a tapping foot, darting eyes, fingers drumming on the tabletop, a knee pumping up and down, a foot shuffling while you are seated, and so on.

◆ Project relaxed energy with a bright expression, a smile, erect but not rigid posture, a sitting position that is slightly forward.

◆ Make and maintain eye contact, but do not stare. Staring communicates an arrogant need to control the situation—or maybe it tells others that you're just plain weird. Eye contact conveys openness and honesty. Avoidance of eye contact conveys insincerity, fear, evasiveness, or maybe just an absence of interest. Afraid that maintaining eye contact will be confused with staring? Smile, adopt an animated expression, and do not hesitate to look away—as long as you come back to the other person's eyes. Maintaining eye contact does not require a glaring, fixed gaze.

◆ Avoid narrowing your eyes. This conveys hostility, disagreement, resentment, or disapproval. Outright squinting suggests total puzzlement: you haven't a clue.

- Downcast eyes suggest shame.

- Raised eyebrows indicate surprise or disbelief, something that may or may not be a negative signal, depending on the situation.

- Tilting your head to one side indicates interest.

- A slightly outthrust chin conveys confidence. Stick out your chin too far, however, and you'll appear pompous and arrogant. A lowered chin conveys defensiveness and insecurity.

- Nodding up and down conveys agreement, whereas shaking the head from side to side conveys disagreement. No surprises here. Just make sure your nonverbal gestures coincide with your words. A young man asks you out for coffee. You answer yes, but shake your head no. What is your *real* answer? What are you thinking? What are you feeling? And what are you making the other person think and feel?

- Scratching your head indicates confusion or disbelief.

- Rubbing the back of your neck suggests disbelief or anxiety.

Safe Move _____

A smile is the single most powerful gesture you can use to make positive, affirmative contact with others. It invites contact and connection.

- Rubbing the forehead indicates confusion.

- Putting your hands anywhere near your mouth or nose conveys extreme nervousness or evasiveness.

- Lip biting is a signal of significant anxiety.

- Pursed lips convey strong resistance to suggestion or great skepticism: a closed mind.

- Sighing is a powerful sign of distress or even hopelessness.

Hand Signals

Many people are self-conscious about their hands, believing that "talking with your hands" is distracting or even "low class" (whatever that means). Actually, your hands are powerful nonverbal instruments of communication. Use them.

Open hands, palms up, suggest honesty and openness. Rubbing the hands together communicates positive expectation. Putting the fingertips of both hands together like a steeple conveys confidence. It is best, however, to avoid fist pounding, stabbing the air with your finger, poking your listener in the chest, crossing your arms in front of your own chest (this conveys defiance, defensiveness, resistance, aggressiveness, or a closed mind), and hand wringing, which is a compelling signal of worry verging on terror.

Reading People

The same nonverbal cues you project are what you should look for in others. Expression and gesture tell you a great deal about how others feel and how you are coming across to them. It's true that listening is the most important aspect of effective communication. Less obvious is another truth: effective listening is done as much with the eyes as with the ears. Listen—and *look*.

- If the person you are talking to tilts his head to one side, you can assume that he is listening intently to what you are saying and is interested.

- Head scratching indicates confusion or disbelief. Take this signal as your cue to pause and ask a question: "I'm not sure I'm making myself clear. Let me put it another way ...."

- If the person to whom you are speaking rubs the back of her head or neck, she may be getting frustrated or impatient. Consider moving on to another topic—or simply moving on.

- If the other person lowers his chin markedly, he may be conveying a degree of defensiveness, suggesting that he has interpreted something you've said as a criticism. If you did not intend to be critical, make an appropriately soothing remark: "Of course, I think you're doing just fine."

- If the other person nods up and down, keep the conversation going in the current vein.

- If something you say provokes a head shake from side to side, be aware that what you have said is being rejected or objected to.

Tackle this directly: "I can see that you don't agree. What's the problem?"

◆ It can be challenging to interpret the meaning of the avoidance of eye contact. Perhaps the other person is just shy. The best response is to be friendly or friendlier.

Victimology 101

Reading others and projecting a confident, positive self-image are important skills for living well in any community, including college. They are also skills you can apply directly to avoiding situations and people who mean trouble.

Spotting Bad Actors

When a cop calls someone a "bad actor," he's not referring to a film star of limited talent, but a person whose intentions and behavior are not good. We are often told to look out for people who "behave suspiciously." But what does that mean? Successful crooks are usually successful because they don't go around looking and acting like criminals; but then, most bad actors are not very successful. A skilled poker player learns how to read his opponents by looking for "tells"—expressions, gestures, habits, and tics that betray the player's hand. You can learn to recognize the typical "tells" of the bad actor, even in a crowd:

◆ He or she often seems preoccupied, perhaps agitated.

◆ When the bad actor speaks, the tone of voice may change abruptly, becoming by turns inappropriately loud or exaggeratedly soft.

◆ Facial expression is often notable. The face of a bad actor may show unusual rage or stress—or, just as notably, an eerie absence of expression: a blankness.

◆ Yes, it's true: the bad actor is often shifty-eyed—the eyes darting about rapidly. Exaggerated narrowing of the eyes also suggests a person with dubious intentions. The gaze of a bad actor may also seem unfocused.

- ◆ Look out for obvious signs of aggression, including verbal outbursts accompanied by emphatic or violent hand gestures.

- ◆ Look out for obvious signs of stress, especially profuse sweating.

The bottom line is to watch out for people whose appearance and behavior are inappropriate to the situation. The bad actor may be too loud or too quiet; he may be strangely aloof and apart, haunting the sidelines instead of participating in the activity around him. He may be inappropriately dressed—wearing a long, heavy coat on a hot day, for example (to conceal a weapon?). He may simply look inappropriate—for example, blank in expression when everyone else is smiling. He may be deliberately rowdy or provocative.

At the very least, read the bad actor—and steer clear. If the appearance and behavior are sufficiently alarming, don't hesitate to alert authorities.

> **Bad Idea!**
>
> Do not approach a suspicious-looking or suspicious-acting person to inquire what's wrong or what's going on. Avoid the person. If his or her actions, demeanor, or even presence is genuinely disturbing to you, call campus security or the police.

Profile of a Victim

Just as you can become adept at spotting bad actors, bad actors are often adept at spotting likely victims. Consider the following scenario.

Jane Doe is a college junior. One evening, she makes her way from class to her car in an enclosed parking garage. She is alone. Her arms are loaded down with books and a laptop computer in an expensive leather carrying case. On her shoulder she carries a bag with a big designer monogram in gold. She is struggling under her load and thinking about a term paper due in just two days. She is preoccupied, visibly lost in thought.

A pair of thieves watch her go into the parking ramp, alone. As she approaches her car, awkwardly setting down her things and fumbling with a key, they strike, grabbing her, holding a knife to her throat, snatching her purse and laptop, as well as a gold chain she wears around her neck. When it's all over, a badly shaken Jane Doe counts herself "lucky" that she was not killed, beaten, or raped—just robbed of several thousand dollars worth of stuff, including a laptop containing class notes, homework, and personal information.

Why was Jane Doe targeted?

Different bad actors may look for different qualities in a potential victim, but, whatever else they look for, all target people who obviously look like they have something worth taking and who appear unfocused, disorganized, distracted—in short, preoccupied.

In criminology and law enforcement, *victimology* is the study of victims of crime, the factors that make one person more likely to be the victim of a crime—and a particular kind of crime—than another. It is an increasingly complex and sophisticated field based on the gathering, collation, and analysis of a large body of data. All you need to know about victimology, however, is that most victims present themselves—in one way or another—as victims. This is not to blame the victim for crime. Make no mistake, the offender, not the victim, is guilty. However, all crimes against persons require at least two people: an offender and a victim. You *can* take steps to avoid appearing like a victim:

◆ Accept the possibility that something bad can happen. The point is not to let this frighten you, but to keep you from becoming wrapped in a cocoon of denial.

◆ Maintain vigilance—relaxed awareness.

◆ Avoid distraction. Avoid preoccupation.

◆ Look alert, focused, and aware.

◆ Get connected with the campus, with your community, and with a circle of good friends and acquaintances. Don't be a loner. Look out for others, and they will look out for you.

◆ Broadcast a positive attitude, including a body language that conveys self-confidence.

◆ Avoid dangerous situations when you can. Stay out of isolated corners of campus. Whenever possible, walk with friends rather than alone, especially after dark.

◆ Don't display your wealth. Ditch the bling. Carry your high-end laptop or iPod as inconspicuously as possible.

◆ Plan. When you are going into a scary situation—such as a parking garage at an off hour—think about what you can do if you are threatened. We'll talk more about some of your best self-defense options in Chapter 15.

◆ Decide to survive. Like all animals, human beings have a strong survival instinct. Tap into it. Resolve to use it.

Accept Responsibility

It's wrong, it's outrageous, to blame the victim of crime for crime. But it's even more dangerous when we refuse to accept responsibility for keeping ourselves safe. Accept the possibility of crime or accident, then make it your business to learn the ways in which you can minimize that possibility.

The Least You Need to Know

◆ Living on campus does not make you immune to accident or crime.

◆ Vigilance—an attitude of relaxed awareness—will help you to avoid becoming a victim of accident or of crime.

◆ Becoming a "people person" will help you develop a connection with the campus community—an important step to staying safe and secure.

◆ Practice positive body language and learn to "read" the body language of others, including potential "bad actors."

2

Scoping Out Schools

In This Chapter

- ◆ Traditional versus urban campuses
- ◆ Staying safe in the rural and small-town campus
- ◆ Coping with the challenges of the urban campus
- ◆ The student as commuter
- ◆ How to get the campus security picture

There are some things in life that can be pursued head-on, without preparation or consideration. The choice of where you go to college is not one of those choices. The stakes are too high should the experience not be a good one. The whole point is to be somewhere that feels right, suits you (and your parents), and provides you with the proper environment in which you can study, learn, and grow.

In Search of an Experience

You have just finished high school. You have some idea about what lies ahead, but not much. The last four years of hard work and dedication have led to the opportunity for a college education—something hard to come by during your parents' time and nearly unreachable for your grandparents. What are you going to do with this chance?

The academic challenges will be sufficiently difficult, but the choice you make on where you attend school will go a long way toward determining your future. In fact, so many choices face you, it will help to have a plan. Think about what you like and what you want. Consider what others have told you, but remember they are not you. Visit different schools and soak in the experience. Talk to students, friends, your high school counselor, and, of course, family. Use your head to determine where your body will be for four years or longer.

Little Black Book

Here are four must-see websites to help you narrow down your college search:

- College Matchmaker at http://apps.collegeboard.com/search/index.jsp
- College Prowler at www.collegeprowler.com
- Peterson's Planner at www.petersons.com
- *U.S. News & World Report* Annual College Guide at http://colleges.usnews.rankingsandreviews.com/usnews/edu/college/rankings/rankindex_brief.php

The Traditional Campus

In days gone by, the traditional college campus was envisioned as a little world apart, planted in a small town or a rural setting. The college was pretty much the town, and the town took what it could from the college. Often, there was a certain level of friction between "townies" and students. Today, relations between "town and gown" tend to be far more positive, because most towns that are home to a college have learned to be proud of the fact, and many colleges—formerly pretty exclusive places—have reached out to the communities that host them. Nevertheless, the realities of the traditional campus are not always pleasant.

Small World or Real World?

Set in its own little world, the traditional small-town or semirural campus may seem remote from the harsh realities of "mainstream" urban life. The fact is that, these days, practically no place is truly remote, and that includes the traditional campus. It is hardly free from the temptations, hardships, and trials that beset the rest of modern civilization. Alcohol, controlled substances—and the opportunities to abuse them—as well as violent crime and other forms of victimization are prevalent everywhere, no matter how idyllic the picture. The campus attracts not just those who want to learn and those who want to teach, but also those who would profit from crime.

The rolling hills or coastal plains in which many traditional campuses are located may harbor drug dealers, thieves, and sexual predators. The geographical isolation of the traditional campus may contribute to the kind of academic experience that appeals to you, but it may also hide threats. On balance, the traditional campus is neither safer nor less safe than a campus located in or near big cities. As always, vigilance is the key. Stay alert, and remain savvy and street smart—even in a place with very few streets.

Hard Fact
According to the U.S. Drug Enforcement Administration (DEA), 6,435 "labs" for the manufacture of methamphetamine ("meth") were seized in 2006, many of them in rural areas. Makers of meth like to work in the country because of the isolation and the availability of numerous abandoned buildings such as farmhouses and barns on remote roads. Anhydrous ammonia, a key ingredient in meth production, is also readily available in rural areas in the form of chemical fertilizer. Meth makers often loot farmers' anhydrous ammonia storage units. The good news is that the 2006 meth seizure figures are well below those of 2005, a year in which 12,484 meth labs were seized. In 2004, there were 17,170 seizures.

Look Closely at the College Community

Transferring from one school to another is hardly unusual, of course, but most students who graduate complete their education at the college or university in which they initially enrolled. This means that when you are choosing a college, you are very likely choosing your home for the next four years. Classes and books will keep you busy for some of that time, but, count on it, there will be a lot left over, and that's why it is important that you scope out the college community while you are still shopping for a place to learn. This is an important step to take whether you are looking at a traditional or an urban campus, but it is absolutely crucial in the case of the traditional campus.

What are you going to do with all your downtime? The campus setting may be quiet and quaint, but what leisure opportunities does "quiet and quaint" afford? As you consider any campus—but especially a traditional campus—pay close attention to what the campus itself offers. It will be your community, your main source of intellectual stimulation, entertainment, relaxation, invigoration, and inspiration. The classes may be just what you want, and the professors may have great reputations, but if the place does not offer a variety of other activities that interest you, chances are you're going to be disappointed, discontent, and bored. Generally speaking, people who are disappointed, discontent, and bored readily find trouble, or it finds them.

As you shop for a school, do not shortchange the nonacademic attractions that appeal to you, including student associations, student government, political clubs, athletics, religious groups, preprofessional organizations, charities, hobby-oriented organizations, arts groups, musical groups, theater groups, and the like. Many campuses offer exciting and rewarding opportunities to volunteer in the community or elsewhere nationally or even internationally. Think about what interests you, and make sure the campuses you're considering offer plenty of it.

Maybe you're really into anime, but your number-one college prospect does not have an anime club. Find out how open the college is to organizing new clubs. Most campuses welcome new ideas and organizations—but some are less welcoming than others. Will it be possible for you to start an anime club after you enroll? Ask questions. Check it out.

Commit to the College Community

It's a great thing to choose a campus that has plenty going on, but your choice means little if, once you are enrolled, you fail to make yourself part of the community.

There are many activities available on traditional campuses that many students never take advantage of. Those student associations, athletic activities, religious groups, and other organizations just mentioned hold many events at which attendance is typically well short of full.

You are part of your campus community. Commit to it. Visit clubs and organizations. Attend meetings, concerts, and athletic events. Get involved. At the very least, you will meet and enjoy others in a safe, relaxing, yet stimulating environment.

Big time college sports are glamorous, commercial, exciting, and mean a lot to a school. But a sport does not have to draw huge crowds paying top-dollar prices to be exciting and entertaining. Even if your campus is small and the athletic teams modest, make it a point to enjoy a match or a race. Take a friend and go. Make a friend and go. The purpose is not to "keep you out of trouble"—though it might just do that—but to help you develop a network of friends and helpers. The more thoroughly you integrate yourself into the campus community, the safer and happier you are likely to be.

Safe Move

Some campuses are way out of the way. If an event requires a road trip, think ahead. There may be some lonely stretches of road. Keep a full tank of gas, a blanket, some emergency supplies, and a set of tools so that you will be able to respond to an unforeseen bad situation. Charge up your cell phone and keep it with you, but be aware that not all rural locations have good cell service. Have a back-up plan and think positively. Don't leave without letting someone know where you are going, when you expect to get there, and when you plan on returning.

Phone Home

Self-reliance is an admirable quality, but, as the poet said, no one is an island. Just because you are physically away from home, your family, and those of your friends who are still at home or have gone to other schools does not mean you can't phone them, write to them, and e-mail them. Staying in touch won't compromise your independence.

If you need some help and support from your parents or others, ask. People actually like to help—and parents relish the feeling of being needed. But don't make it a habit to phone only when you need cash or a favor. That's a bad idea. If you keep in touch regularly, just to share news and to say "I love you," your calls will always be welcome.

The Urban Campus

If there are great colleges and universities in little towns and out in the boonies, there are also wonderful schools in the cities. Your choice of institution may depend mainly on what the school offers academically, on the financial demands it makes (or incentives it offers), on religious affiliation, and so on. It may have little or nothing to do with where the school happens to be located. On the other hand, some students really want to go to a traditional campus, whereas others can't stand the thought of being away from the bright lights and the big city.

It's a fact that many of the new or growing schools are in urban settings. Many colleges and universities use their urban setting as a positive draw to attract top students and top faculty. The urban campus offers great opportunities for expanding your college experience, but this location also presents a set of problems you need to be aware of.

All of the challenges associated with urban living are magnified on the urban campus. There are petty crime, homelessness, vagrancy, vandalism, and auto theft, as well as robbery, rape, and even murder. The campus is not only *not* immune to these ills, but may well attract predators who see a concentration of potential victims.

Protecting the Campus

No urban campus survives without facing the realities that surround it. Most city-based colleges and universities have long ago prepared themselves to deal with big-city problems. Campus police departments in urban schools are usually highly trained and very professional. You may notice that the campus police even patrol parts of the downtown area that are outside the campus. The jurisdiction of most urban university police departments usually extends some distance beyond the boundaries of campus. There is a reason for this, since pushing the crime somewhere else is a most effective law enforcement tactic.

Learn to respect and rely on the campus cops as you would on the city police or the county sheriff. They are the guardians of your community. Report to the campus police any suspicious activity.

Savvy homebuyers check out all services before moving into a new town, suburb, or neighborhood, and that includes the local police force. You should do the same when you are in the process of choosing schools. Begin with the institution's website. How much does it tell you about the campus public safety, or police, department? How seriously does it take the job of protecting the campus community? When you tour a campus, ask to speak to a public safety officer. Talk to him or her about your safety concerns. Ask him or her what the biggest campus security problems are and how they're being dealt with.

> **Bad Idea!**
>
> Never take a stranger back to your room, your car, your dorm, or any other campus location. You are not just looking out for you; you are looking out for your fellow students. If you see someone on the street who is obviously disoriented or confused, injured, unconscious, or seriously ill, call 911 to summon aid.

Homelessness

Homelessness is an issue facing most cities. The homeless often gravitate toward urban campus settings because of the relative safety they find there and because of the well-meaning generosity of the student population. Most students tend to be compassionate people, but it's important to temper the urge to help with an awareness that among the homeless are criminals, drug abusers, and the mentally ill, some of whom are dangerous. The best way to help the homeless you may encounter in or near campus is to give aid as a member of an organized, supported campus effort. This is most effective for the people you are trying to help, and it is safest for you and the entire college community. If an organized effort does not exist on your campus, consider working to get one started. Don't try to work alone.

Commuter Considerations

Many students attending urban campuses are commuters. You don't have to live on campus to fit into campus life. As a commuter student you will have a combination of experiences, including those of the typical college student as well as those of the typical urban commuter. If public transportation is unavailable and you must commute by car, parking may well be your biggest daily headache. Whether you park on or off campus, you will need to protect yourself and your valuables by following the recommendations in Chapter 7.

Commuter Parking

Crimes associated with the automobile are all too common and rarely prosecuted vigorously. The thief, therefore, sees remarkably little downside associated with the crimes of auto theft and "entering auto" (breaking into a car to steal its contents). Many criminals tend to regard police action against them in these acts as little more than a minor inconvenience.

This doesn't mean that *you* have to be a victim, however. In addition to reviewing Chapter 7, be a proactive commuter from the get-go. Decide whether or not it's worth buying that fancy new car. There are any number of good reasons to hold off on that purchase until after graduation, the financial burden and the lure to criminals among them.

Never leave valuables in plain view when you park, and always lock your doors. Park in well-lit and heavily used parking areas. You've heard of the cliché of the absent-minded professor, but be aware that the mind of a college student can also wander—far, far away. Typically, when you are parking, your mind is already in class. Better to keep your mind on the present moment, where it belongs. Take careful note of where you parked. In a lot or a garage, note the space number, section number, and level number. Write these down. Then walk briskly and with a purposeful stride to your destination. When it's time to return to your car, walk with the same attitude. Never give the appearance of aimlessly wandering in search of your vehicle. Remember: crooks target people who appear lost, confused, and generally unaware. They understand the value of a surprise attack. And who is easier to surprise than someone whose mind and body are clearly not in the same place at the same time?

Public Transportation

For getting to and from many urban campuses, public transportation is the ideal option. It allows you to avoid the inconvenience and risk of parking, it's friendlier to the environment, and it's ultimately more economical for you. Chapter 7 has advice on using public transportation safely and confidently.

Riding public transportation is almost always safer than driving your own car. Nevertheless, on a bus or a train, you are in public, and you are riding with every element of society. In cities where public transportation is difficult to use or has a bad reputation, the percentage of unsavory characters is generally higher.

Investigate the public transportation options in your community. Look at websites, read the newspaper, and take a good hard look for yourself. Are the buses or trains well maintained? Are they full? Empty? Somewhere in between? Are police officers present in and around public transportation facilities? A police presence is a good thing. It is *not* a sign of the presence of crime, but of a proactive attitude toward preventing crime. Bike patrols, vehicle patrols, and walking patrols are all desirable on a public transit system.

You can enhance your safety on public transportation by observing the following rules:

♦ Travel during the busier times of day.

♦ When you can, travel with a buddy or in groups.

♦ Avoid traveling at off hours, especially late at night.

♦ Avoid identifying yourself as a student.

♦ Review Chapter 1 and check out Chapter 15 for tips on how to ensure that you don't make yourself look like a victim.

♦ Stay alert to your surroundings.

Your "Safety School"

Getting into the college or university of your choice can be a highly competitive contest. Prudent students target one, two, or more dream schools, but they also apply to at least one "safety school"—an acceptable alternative they are confident will take them if the target schools say no.

No one is all that thrilled about ending up at their safety school, but maybe it's time to start thinking of that phrase in an altogether different way—because even your dream school should also be your safety school.

Remember, in choosing a college or university, you are picking the place that will most likely be your home for at least four years. Few of us would deliberately choose to live in a place that makes us uncomfortable or fearful, that makes us feel perpetually unsafe. Most students choose a school on the basis of the following very reasonable criteria:

- Degrees offered
- Majors and minors available
- Faculty reputation
- Overall reputation for quality
- Numerical ranking
- Location
- Size of the student population
- Public versus private
- Costs
- Financial assistance packages
- Campus resources, such as labs, libraries, and so on
- Career placement success
- Student body, including racial and cultural diversity and gender diversity
- Social life, including the role of Greek organizations

- Athletic programs

- Religious affiliations—or the absence thereof

- Housing options

- Realistic odds of being admitted

All of these are important. But the one criterion that is rarely included on the list is the most important of all. It is, in fact, a matter of life and death. *How safe is the school?*

Bad Idea!

Failing to include safety and security on your list of campus criteria when you are looking for a college or university is a bad idea. What is more important than protecting your life?

On the Web, in the Brochure

Get all the information you can on the schools that interest you. In addition to finding the facts on the kinds of decision issues we've just listed, be sure to get the safety picture of your target campus.

Not too many years ago, automobile ads never mentioned safety. Looks, horsepower, a leather interior, and a boatload of options were what the consumer wanted and what the manufacturers advertised. More recently, however, safety has become a top selling point and is often the chief focus of ads. Much the same is true about the way colleges and universities present themselves to the world. It used to be that parents as well as students took for granted that they would be safe in school, that a college or university was somehow immune to crime, accident, and disaster. Of course, that was never the case, but it was a pervasive and comforting illusion. Any number of recent incidents and tragedies have finally driven the hard truths home.

You should have no difficulty finding information about a prospective institution's safety programs—including campus police, campus counseling, and student health services—on that institution's website and in its other promotional literature. If you cannot readily locate this information, you may have identified a serious weakness in the school's approach to safety issues. If your heart is still set on this institution, make a phone call to the public information office, the dean of admissions, the dean of students, or the campus safety office itself. Ask questions. If you visit the campus, make sure that the campus police and student health center are included on your tour.

The Clery Act

In 1986, Jeanne Clery, a Lehigh (Pennsylvania) University freshman, was raped and murdered in her campus residence hall. The parents of this 19-year-old did not simply grieve. When they learned that students hadn't been informed of the 38 violent crimes that had taken place on the Lehigh campus in the three years before their daughter's murder, they joined with other campus crime victims to persuade Congress to enact the Crime Awareness and Campus Security Act, also called the Disclosure of Campus Security Policy and Campus Crime Statistics Act, but best known as the Clery Act, which was signed into law in 1990.

This federal statute requires all colleges and universities that participate in federal financial aid programs to maintain and to disclose information about crime on and near their campuses. The U.S. Department of Education monitors compliance with the law and has the authority to impose civil penalties, up to $27,500 per violation, against institutions for each infraction of reporting requirements. The department can even suspend institutions from participating in federal student financial aid programs.

By October 1 annually, institutions are required to publish and distribute a formal campus security report to current and prospective students and employees. They may publish the report online as well as in printed format.

Each report must provide crime statistics for the prior three years and include policy statements regarding the institution's safety and security measures, campus crime prevention programs, and (in particular) the procedures that are to be followed in the investigation and prosecution of alleged sex offenses. The law requires that the campus police or security department maintain a public log of all crimes reported directly to the department as well as any other crimes of which the department is made aware. The log must include information for the most recent 60 days, and each log entry must contain the nature, date, time, and general location of each offense as well as the disposition of the complaint, if known. Information older than 60 days must be retained and made available on request within two business days. The crime logs are required to be kept for seven years, three years following the publication of the last annual security report. The Clery Act also requires institutions to give timely warnings of crimes that represent a threat to the safety of students or employees.

All institutions that participate in federal financial assistance programs are required to keep the most recent three years of crime statistics that have occurred on campus, in residential halls, in noncampus college or university buildings, or on public property near the campus. Statistics are maintained on criminal homicide (murder and non-negligent manslaughter), negligent manslaughter, sexual offenses, robbery, aggravated assault, burglary, arson, and motor vehicle theft as well as arrests and/or disciplinary referrals for liquor-law violations, drug-law violations, and illegal weapons possession.

The Clery Act gives you a powerful instrument for evaluating the safety picture at any school you are likely to apply to, but before you assume that the act guarantees full disclosure, keep in mind that the system still involves people. The penalties may be severe for failure to disclose, but it is still the case that no school likes to report bad things, especially with so much riding on such popular college rankings as those published annually in *U.S. News and World Report*, and, as with most laws, there is sufficient complexity in this one to have left a few loopholes open. For instance, internal disciplinary actions not resulting in arrests are supposed to be reported and count toward the statistics; nevertheless, some administrators manage to find wiggle room in this reporting demand.

> ### Hard Fact
>
> The Clery Act singles out hate crimes for special treatment. Colleges and universities are required to indicate if any of the crimes reported were classified as a hate crime, an assault (or other crime) in which the victim was targeted on account of his or her race, religion, nationality, or sexual orientation. (The murder of Jeanne Clery did not fall into the category of hate crime.)

This said, most schools are honest and do their best to follow the letter of the law. Look at the statistics for your prospective school online. There should be a link to the Clery stats on the school's website, usually through the public safety, security, or police web page.

When considering the stats, remember that reported incidents do not necessarily indicate a crime wave. The fact that incidents are honestly reported usually means the administration is facing up to something unpleasant, but real. Sometimes the safest place to be is the place where crime is recognized as a reality and measures are taken to address the issue.

Be Prepared, Not Scared

Crime is a feature of our society, and since the college campus is undeniably a part of society, crime is a feature of the college campus as well. The biggest danger you face from crime is clinging to the fiction that, somehow, the campus is immune and exempt. It is not. In some ways, the dangers may be lessened because of more intensely focused security and the closeness of the academic community. In other ways, however, the dangers may be magnified, since there is always a group of predators who see a concentration of students as a pool of likely victims.

Don't be scared, be prepared. Stay aware, practice common sense, and, above all, count yourself as a member of the community. Stay in touch with others. Work together to help make your campus a safe place.

The Least You Need to Know

- ◆ Traditional campuses are located in small towns or urban settings, whereas urban campuses are integrated into cities. Neither setting is immune to crime.

- ◆ The relative peace and quiet of a traditional campus does not guarantee safety. You may feel that you are in a world apart, but you are still very much in the world, with all its opportunities as well as challenges.

- ◆ Urban campuses are really urban neighborhoods and should be regarded with appropriate vigilance.

- ◆ Commuting to and from campus—like commuting to and from work—requires extra care and caution.

- ◆ Take advantage of the requirements of the Clery Act to get the safety picture of any college or university you are considering attending.

Part 2

On Campus and Off

This part begins with a chapter on surviving life in a dorm. It goes on to a frank assessment of the opportunities and liabilities of the fraternity and sorority experience, then provides chapters on keeping *your* property *yours* and on avoiding Internet identity theft and online assaults on your personal safety. Chapter 7 takes you out onto the campus and off campus, providing valuable tips for staying safe when you're out and about. Chapter 8 is a fact-filled discussion of alcohol and drugs from the standpoint of your health as well as your relationship to the law. Part 2 concludes with a special chapter on spring break—and how to come home from it alive, well, and without a criminal record.

Chapter 3

Dorm Rules

In This Chapter

- Choosing a roommate
- Agreeing on ground rules
- Creating a safe dormitory community
- Dealing with the RA
- Dorm room visitors
- What to do in an emergency

For most college students, the dormitory is both a first experience of living away from the family and a first immersion in communal living. Dorm life can be fun and rewarding, a great way to make new friends, to broaden cultural and intellectual horizons, and to learn a lot about people. It can also be a tough test of tolerance and maturity. Whatever else dorm life is, it forces people to share both space and responsibility. To be successful, even tolerable, it requires a careful mix of sharing and privacy—and always a commitment to watching out for one another.

Choosing Roommates

As you'll see in Chapter 10, when it comes to college roommates, sometimes you get to choose, sometimes you don't. That's the name of the game, and it's a lot like the rest of life. Whether your roommates are the result of choice or chance, they will be closer to you than your own family for a big part of your school year. Some have the homemaking skills of Martha Stewart, some sell drugs out of your room, and some hang their underwear on the drawer knobs, turned inside out to wear the next day.

Diversity and complexity are great things about people, but it's hard to bear that in mind when someone else—over and over again—tramples on your expectations of what an ideal roommate should be. Be flexible, keep a sense of humor, but know where to draw the line. That line should be drawn somewhere short of criminal behavior.

A Word on Criteria

As we'll consider further in Chapter 10, you may have the opportunity to pick your roommate based upon some selection process your school allows you to participate in. You may think you know what you want, but the truth is that you probably don't. Choosing a roommate based upon a person's taste in music or sports teams affiliation is no more scientific than getting together because you both have green hair. Nevertheless, basing your choice on a few superficialities might be fun, and that's all right. After all, you're not going to marry your roommate. Then again, for at least two semesters, you are going to spend as much time together as if you really were married.

> **Bad Idea!**
>
> Don't choose a roommate on impulse. Just because you have similar taste in music or both enjoy martial arts movies does not mean you'll be compatible. Delve deeper, if you have the opportunity. Take the time to fill out any housing questionnaires that may come your way. Getting stuck with a roommate you don't like is usually not the end of the world, but why not try to avoid it?

Take time to decide on the things that really matter to you. Separate these from issues on which you can easily compromise. Having taken time for this exercise in introspection, go and make your selection. Chapter 10 will help.

Take time choosing a roommate, but don't agonize. And rest assured that your prospective roommate is at least as unsettled about you as you are about him or her.

Ask the Basic Questions

Conflict is a part of just about any relationship. Chapter 10 talks about dealing with conflict—especially with roommates—but it's always best to try to avoid major causes of conflict before a dispute actually develops.

For your own safety and peace of mind, ask your prospective roommate point-blank how he or she feels about alcohol and drugs. Know where you stand. Legally, you and your roommate or roommates are in joint possession and control of a room. That means that you may be held accountable for any contraband—drugs, alcohol, whatever—found in your room, whether you brought it in or not. Being "held accountable" can mean subjecting yourself to college or university disciplinary action or it can mean something that comes down a lot heavier: arrest and trial for possession of a controlled substance.

Chapter 10 has more questions to ask—about study habits, quiet time, sleep time, nocturnal visits from significant others, and unending visits from bored siblings who crave a taste of the big-time college experience. To these, you may not get the answer you want, and you may not get any answer at all. How you deal with this is up to you, but concerning issues of drugs and alcohol, you have an absolute right to an answer and to making sure you get the answer you want. Take responsibility for yourself by communicating to your roommate the fact that you are not going to take responsibility for his or her behavior.

Living the Golden Rule

You don't have to be a Christian to recognize the wisdom of the Golden Rule as a way of getting along in a community. How should you behave? Just "do unto others as you would have them do unto you." It's the basis of morality in just about every religion or culture: treat others as you would like to be treated.

Your fellow dorm residents are the closest members of your campus community. Treat them as you would like them to treat you. This includes accepting some responsibility for their safety and welfare. Fortunately, doing so does not involve much sacrifice, since looking out for your roommates and the others in your residence hall begins with looking out for yourself.

The things you do to behave responsibly and safely protect you and, in so doing, protect those around you as well.

Staying safe is mostly a matter of common sense, and the commonest of commonsense actions you can take is always to lock the door to your dorm room. If outer doors in the residence hall lock when you close them, don't prop them open as a "courtesy" to others. The doors lock because only those who have keys—i.e., the authorized residents—are supposed to be able to get in.

> **Hard Fact**
>
> Residence hall violations of rules on liquor tops the list of most college and university crime reports. Drug abuse complaints come next, followed by sexual assault.

Don't smoke in your room. This is a health as well as a fire hazard.

Follow the rules on alcohol consumption in residence halls.

Be considerate when others are studying or sleeping. Make an extra effort to avoid waking a sleeping roommate.

Don't bring strangers into your room. Doing so risks your life, but, because your room is not just *your* room, but a room in a building shared by many others, it risks everyone's lives, property, and well-being.

Who are strangers? A stranger is anyone you don't know very, very well, including the busboy at the all-you-can-drink-for-$2 margarita bar and the hitchhiking backpacker from Europe with the short skirt and the beguiling accent.

"I gotta be me," the old song goes. And there may be some truth in that. But in a dorm, you are also part of a community, a community knitted together by shared responsibilities and a mutual commitment to one another's safety.

Safe Room

You share responsibility for the safety and welfare of everyone in your dorm community, but that does not mean that you should—or even can—take responsibility for everything everyone else does. Responsibility starts with yourself and the space you control: your room.

Lock Up

The best way to keep yourself, your roommate, your stuff, and your room safe is to lock your door. How obvious is that? To many college students, apparently not obvious at all. Getting students to lock their doors is the simplest and most effective way to deter crime on any campus, yet students are notorious for leaving doors unlocked, propping doors open, giving out keys to just about anyone, or even leaving a ground-floor window open so some late-arriving guest will have open access to their room. Doing these things puts everyone in jeopardy— something you have no right to do.

Please Don't Burn Down the Dorm

Once you lock your door, play safe with fire. Mishaps with open burners, candles, and burning incense cause most fires in dormitory settings. Follow all published or posted fire safety rules. Even if the rules in your residence hall don't explicitly prohibit candles, it is best to avoid all open flames. Face it: candles really don't go all that far to make the average dorm room a more romantic place. You'd need a miracle.

The same goes for all heating appliances, such as electric space heaters, toasters, hot plates, and coffeemakers. Unplug all of these when they are not in use and especially when you leave your room.

Safe Move

Most dormitories prohibit or limit the use of candles and other sources of open flame, as well as the use of hot plates, electric heaters, coffeemakers, and the like. Breaking these rules is dangerous and selfish. Even if candles and various electric heating appliances are permitted, never leave them unattended.

Fires in dorms are deadly serious business. Participate with your full attention in fire drills. If your dorm does not regularly conduct fire drills, ask your resident advisor (RA) why. It's your life that's at stake.

Take all fire alarms seriously. Just because you don't see fire or smell smoke doesn't mean you're experiencing a false alarm. Don't hide under the covers when you hear the alarm. Assume that you are being called on to save your life. If your roommates are asleep, wake them up.

It's a bad idea to set off a false alarm. Of course, it's illegal. Add to that stupid, dangerous, moronic, and evil. No one has the right to play with your life, which means that you have no right to play with the lives of others.

"Neighborhood" Watch

Locking your own door and making sure you don't set your room on fire are all about carefully minding your own business. The next step is to mind the business of those around you as well.

What's the best insurance money *can't* buy? The eyes and ears of a nosy neighbor.

The little old lady who makes it a habit to watch the world from her front porch is usually an effective deterrent to crime, a very credible witness, and an even more effective early warning system. She may not understand everything that's going on, but she certainly can recognize unusual activity. Something of the same principle applies to campus life. An abundance of witnesses—people coming, going, and *watching*—provide a measure of safety in a community whose members are aware and involved.

So Be a Little Old Lady

Learn to become the little old lady on her porch: a good witness and a contributing protector of your community. You don't have to be told what looks routine, normal, and right versus what appears out of place and suspicious. You know the differences instinctively. Anything that makes you look twice, that makes you think, that raises the hairs on the back of your neck is worth reporting.

Why is that van pulled up to the dorm, with people you don't recognize taking furniture and a television out the door?

Who is that stranger behind the bushes, along the path runners use during morning workouts? What's he doing there, anyway?

If you see strange people nosing about the residence hall, use your cell phone to call campus security. Do it right away.

Bear Witness

A man runs out of the residence hall, a small flat-screen TV under his arm. What do you do?

That depends, first, on what you think you can do—safely. It is almost certainly not a good idea to run after him, at least not alone. You could start yelling and gathering a posse of bystanders to give chase. Or you could just bear witness. Watch. Absorb the details. Prepare yourself to answer the following:

- ◆ What happened?
- ◆ When did it happen?
- ◆ Who did you see?
- ◆ How many were there?
- ◆ What did the perpetrator(s) do?
- ◆ What did the perpetrator(s) look like?
- ◆ Male or female?
- ◆ How old?

- ◆ What race?

- ◆ What clothing?

- ◆ Did he/she/they say anything?

- ◆ How did he/she/they get away? On foot? By car?

- ◆ What kind of car?

- ◆ What was the license plate number?

Call 911 and report the crime. Deliver all the details you can.

If a suspect or suspects are subsequently arrested, you may be called upon to identify them. Later, if they are brought to trial, you may be called to court as a witness. Either of these things may take you far outside of your comfort zone, and that's too bad, but acting responsibly is not always comfortable. When you find yourself in a position either to stand up and contribute or to choose not to do so, be aware that the second choice may be more comfortable in the short run, but it lets yourself and the campus community down. And that, in the long run, is downright painful.

The RA

The resident advisor—the RA—is a complex creature. He or she is supposed to be your first resource in any question or problem that arises in the residence hall, and most RAs are indeed eager to help. Moreover, they have the great advantage of being on-site, close to the problem geographically as well as culturally. After all, the RA is a student like you.

And therein lies the chief limitation of the whole RA system.

Many RAs rise wonderfully to their responsibilities, but some—probably quite a few—are neither more nor less than students who have been assigned responsibilities beyond their competence or, in some cases, beyond even their interest.

Competence is limited by the innate ability of the individual, his or her level of maturity, and the often meager training provided by the school. Interest ranges from a sincere desire to be helpful, to "make a difference," down to doing no more than pocketing the stipend or housing allowance that goes with the RA job. In many cases, an RA may get a lot more out of the deal than he or she puts into it.

Get to know your RA. Give him or her the benefit of the doubt. Begin by assuming he or she is driven by the very highest motives. But never rely on the RA as your sole guide and chief salvation.

Use the System—Don't Let It Use You

The problem with the resident advisor system is that administrators as well as dorm residents tend to heap far too much on the RA. Some schools even begin the internal judicial process with a report from the RA, who is expected to monitor and police the behavior of other students.

Some RAs do a better job than others. Certainly, most mean well. Sometimes, the system works—and even works rather well. Nevertheless, the point to remember is that you need to take care of yourself first—which, in a dorm situation, is also the best way to look out for others as well.

Do not rely on the RA or anyone else to protect you or your interests. If you have a problem with someone or something, report it through the proper channels, beginning with the RA—if that's what the rules say. Perhaps you won't have to go any further than the RA. But don't assume that will be the case. If you don't see a resolution to the problem, keep pressing.

 **Bad Idea!**

People who "suffer in silence" are often those who, sooner or later, explode. Screaming, yelling, making threats, or starting a fistfight is always a very bad idea. Speak up before matters get out of hand, and never do anything to hurt yourself or others.

If you have a dispute with a roommate, read Chapter 10 and do your very best to work out the problem with the other person. In most cases, this is the quickest and most satisfactory route to a resolution. If this fails, go to the RA—but don't feel you must stop with him or her. Cooperation and compromise are essential in any community, but that doesn't mean you can't complain when something isn't right. In fact, in the campus environment, the more you complain about some legitimate grievance, the more likely you are to see a satisfactory outcome. This may not seem like a nice and polite way to be, but it's the way to get things done when you get no satisfaction at the level of the RA.

As a last resort, involve your parents. Nothing places fear in the heart of a college administrator like a phone call, or even worse, a visit, from a concerned parent—or, more to the point, an irate mother.

Find the Balance

Stand up for yourself, even if you have to get your parents to help. But before you escalate an issue or a dispute to this point, decide how much you can give. Ultimately, your welfare depends on that of others in the community. If everyone behaves selfishly, no one will be satisfied. Find a balance between what you are willing to tolerate and what you really need to change.

Be My Guest

The accommodations in most dorm rooms fall short of the presidential suite in a five-star hotel. Far short, in fact. Nevertheless, you may find that a surprising number of people are eager to share your room, at least for a time. These include brothers, sisters, cousins, girlfriends or boyfriends, friends, and maybe a lot of people you don't even think of as good friends. Your roommate may well have a similar entourage.

Once you are in close quarters, it can be a shock to discover that you don't know many of these people as well as you thought you did, especially if you or they are drifting in the haze of alcohol or other substances that promote bad decisions.

In the moment, it's often difficult to say no to someone. For that reason, you and your roommate or roommates should develop a policy concerning overnight guests—and, what can be more difficult, stick to it. Agree with your roommates that the policy will stand and will not be bent or broken.

The bedrock of any guest policy should be this: absolutely no strangers in your room. Ever. Strangers are people you don't know. You don't know the student who flunked out and now needs a place to stay. You don't know the girl who doesn't want to go home and stay with her grandmother. You don't know the homeless guy on the corner who is very cold tonight and just wants to share your floor.

Most roommates can agree on a policy that counts a brother or sister coming to visit as an acceptable guest. Likewise a close friend from high school. But things get more complicated with boyfriends and girlfriends, especially when your roommate likes walking around less than fully clothed.

Work out the policy in advance, before it becomes a last-minute issue and creates trouble for you, your roommate, and a potential guest—who is standing in your room, bags in hand, at 3:30 in the morning.

Some schools do the visitation policy making for you, narrowly prescribing who can stay overnight and who cannot. These days, however, the general movement is toward greater freedom for resident students. Just because that is the case, if your roommate objects to your having certain guests, you can't whine that "there's no rule against it." In the absence of a school rule, you *and* your roommate must make and agree on the rules. Conflict thrives in a vacuum.

Who *Is* That Guy, Anyway?

It bears repeating: *never let a stranger into your room.* That's not just a good policy, it's a policy absolutely necessary for your safety—even your survival—and that of everyone else in your residence hall.

If your school is even marginally concerned about security, the people who do the hiring will have run criminal background checks on all persons who have access to student rooms. This includes campus police officers as well as security, maintenance, housekeeping, and residence hall staff. It is, however, highly unlikely that anybody at the school ever ran a criminal background check on the person sleeping in the bed next to you. (Nobody ran one on *you*, did they?)

Even after half the semester has flown by, you probably hardly know your roommate. It's easy to make certain assumptions about him or her. You are law abiding. You come from a decent family. You attend this school. Therefore, the same must be true about your roommate.

Safe Move _____

If your roommate engages in behavior that concerns, worries, or frightens you, go directly to the RA—and tell the RA that you intend to talk with the housing office. If the behavior is clearly dangerous or illegal, report directly to campus security. If you feel that you are in immediate danger, leave the room, get help, and call campus security or 911.

Maybe. But don't close your eyes to behavior that signals trouble or that *is* trouble. Look out for the use of controlled substances; the presence of shady visitors; an excessive demand for privacy; an interest in violent or otherwise disturbing pornography, either online or in print. Being a good roommate often requires the cutting of lots and lots of slack, but you should never feel obligated to tolerate any behavior that is illegal or that you believe puts you in danger.

Guarding the Gate

In college, you don't live alone. That can be a royal pain sometimes, but it's also a good thing. Although your safety is ultimately your own responsibility, there are plenty of people who've got your back. The presence of a genuine campus police force rather than an unarmed band of "rent-a-cops" says a great deal about your school's attitude toward campus safety.

The professionalism of campus police departments has dramatically increased in the last several years. The challenges facing campus safety agencies have become so complex that, in many cases, the campus police are even more highly trained than the local police. If your school has a force of full-time professional police officers, count that as a very positive thing.

Safe Move _____

When you shop for a school, pay at least as much attention to the security force the institution offers as to its faculty.

These days, the secure campus features some form of controlled access, visitor check-in, perimeter patrols, well-lighted areas, emergency call boxes, multiple-staffed security shifts, and a generally safety-conscious attitude.

What's your part in all of this?

Cooperate with the campus police. Make use of all security measures rather than trying to compromise or defeat them. Don't sign in strangers. Don't prop open doors. Don't give out security codes. Don't vouch for people you don't know.

Stuff Happens—Better Make a Plan

Every residence hall should have an evacuation plan in case of fire or other emergency. Make sure that you're familiar with the plan and that, in an emergency, you listen for instructions and follow them.

This said, never rely on rules or the help of others. A fire or other emergency can bring instant chaos, especially at night in a building housing hundreds. Your best chance for survival is to take responsibility for yourself and to be prepared:

- ◆ You and your roommate(s) should each have a flashlight—with fresh batteries.

- ◆ With your roommate(s), walk through and around your residence hall. Familiarize yourselves with all of the exits and stairways. Identify the nearest exit.

- ◆ Ensure that no emergency exits are ever blocked or otherwise made inaccessible or unusable. Report any blocked emergency exits to your RA or campus security.

- ◆ Agree on a buddy system with your roommate(s). In an emergency, agree that you will look out for each other. Make an exit plan.

- ◆ Your exit plan should include a meeting place outside of the building. Agree that, in case of an emergency evacuation, you will meet there.

- ◆ In the event of a fire or other emergency evacuation, always use stairways instead of elevators. There's a very high probability of a power outage that will strand the building's elevators. Avoid them.

It's unhealthy to obsess about disaster, but it can be downright fatal to refuse to think about it at all. Know your building, and make a plan to leave it—quickly and safely—in the event of an emergency. Participate seriously in all fire drills. In the event of an emergency, listen for instructions and follow them. But remember, your safety and survival depend first and last on you. Remember, too, that the steps you take to keep yourself safe will help to keep those who share your room and your residence hall safe as well.

The Least You Need to Know

- Give serious thought to the choice of a roommate, then work together to agree on ground rules that will help you avoid unnecessary conflict and keep you both safe and comfortable.

- Selfish behavior is unsafe behavior, but looking out for yourself responsibly also helps make everyone safer.

- Make use of the resident advisor (RA) but don't rely on him or her to solve all of your problems. Strike a balance between compromise and getting exactly what you want.

- Do not tolerate illegal or dangerous behavior from a roommate. Contact your RA as well as more senior officials, including the campus police.

- Work out with your roommate(s) a plan for evacuation in the event of a fire or other emergency.

Chapter 4

Greek World

In This Chapter

- ◆ The pluses and minuses of Greek life
- ◆ The role of alcohol and drugs
- ◆ Getting to the truth about Greek life
- ◆ Hazing—what it is and why it's bad
- ◆ The connection to rape and sexual exploitation
- ◆ Group behavior and individual accountability

In America, college fraternities and sororities, officially known as Greek letter societies, trace their ancestry to the colonial "Flat Hat Club" of William and Mary College (in Williamsburg, Virginia), which came into existence about 1750, but it was the Kappa Alpha Society, popularly known as Northern K.A., founded in 1825 at Union College in Schenectady, New York, that's considered the oldest existing social fraternity. For this reason and for the other Greek letter fraternities Union College soon spawned, the school today bears the title of "Mother of Fraternities."

Plenty of alumni—former frat brothers and sorority sisters—consider that title an honor. But others, including some educators, parents, students, and even some former Greek letter society members, deem the honor dubious at best. Fraternities—and to a lesser degree, sororities—have a checkered past and a controversial present reputation.

The Good, the Bad, the Oh So Ugly

Even critics of the "Greek system" acknowledge that membership in Greek letter organizations has demonstrated benefits. Various studies have suggested that membership increases the likelihood that students will remain in college through graduation. Fraternity or sorority membership typically broadens the range of a student's acquaintances and friends and provides a support network—a community—on campus. All Greek letter organizations have academic standards that members must maintain to remain in the organization, and many fraternities and sororities offer tutoring, study halls, study groups, and so on to aid academic performance. Some educators believe that Greek organizations have a positive influence on developing their members' leadership skills, encouraging members not only to become active in the leadership of the fraternity or sorority, but in other campus organizations as well. Fraternity and sorority members are often active volunteers in service organizations and charities, and many Greek organizations sponsor their own national philanthropies.

The Lifetime Benefits of Greek Life

Greek letter societies often offer important benefits for the long term, including networking after graduation, which, depending on the fraternity or sorority, may open doors in a career or profession. On average, Greek alumni enjoy higher income levels than students who were not affiliated with Greek letter organizations during college. More difficult to quantify is the impact of fraternity membership on creating lifelong friendships that may well aid future careers. Finally, schools with greater participation in the Greek system enjoy higher rates of alumni giving.

Another Point of View

In an August 2006 study titled "Fraternity Membership and Binge Drinking" published by the National Bureau of Economic Research, University of South Florida economist Jeffrey S. DeSimone forthrightly declared that "although fraternities serve a variety of functions, the predominant activity with which they are associated is the consumption of alcohol." DeSimone points out that these organizations "often connote a culture of heavy drinking, as famously portrayed in the movie *Animal House*" and further states that "anecdotal evidence" as well as "objective data confirm that fraternity members drink more heavily than do non-members." The 1995 National College Health Risk Behavior Survey found that the rate of binge drinking—which the survey defined as consuming at least five alcoholic beverages within the span of a few hours at least once in the past month—was 69 percent among fraternity members and 42 percent among nonmembers.

> ### Little Black Book
>
> *Animal House*, released back in 1978, endures as the classic caricature of Greek life. If you've somehow managed to reach college age without having seen this film, rent a DVD. Not only is it hilarious, it will show you everything your parents fear fraternity membership is all about.

In short, whatever else most fraternities and sororities are—whatever their very real benefits—they are drinking clubs, which, moreover, tend to create a climate in which binge drinking is, if not encouraged, at the very least facilitated. Although heavy drinking is somewhat less prevalent in sororities than in fraternities, it is still practiced at a higher rate than it is among nonsorority students. Along with heavier-than-average drinking, drug use is higher in fraternities and sororities than it is in the general college population.

A little later in this chapter, we will have more to say about binge drinking and other forms of substance abuse as they are related to Greek life, but we need to observe here that drinking and abusing drugs are also associated with another controversial aspect of fraternity and sorority culture: hazing.

Frat and Sorority Myths and Realities

Browse any number of fraternity and sorority websites on the Internet, and you are apt to find various lists of "myths and realities." Greek letter organizations are definitely playing defense these days, but the fact is that ascertaining the truth about Greek life can be pretty difficult. Critics have nothing good to say about fraternities, and supporters are unwilling to concede that there are any real problems.

Even getting Greek membership numbers—something that would seem a simple matter of fact—is difficult. There is a general impression on most campuses that Greek membership is on the decline, but this is an impression various fraternity websites condemn as a myth. The fact is that in 1995, the National College Health Risk Behavior Survey found that more than 18 percent of 18- to 24-year-old full-time four-year college students were fraternity members. In 2001, the Harvard College Alcohol Study pegged membership at 12 percent of 17- to 25-year-old four-year college students.

What should college students make of these numbers? From a national perspective, Greek letter society members are a decided minority. That should give the lie to the proposition that you *absolutely have to* join a fraternity or sorority to get ahead in college. Most college students are not members, and there is some evidence that membership, on the whole, has been declining. Yet it is also true that Greek life is far more important on some campuses than on others. Fraternities and sororities may play very important roles in the school you choose to attend.

Many fraternities fight the *Animal House* stereotype, claiming that each fraternity and sorority is unique—some a bit on the wild side, while others are more serious and sedate. Greek letter societies also often protest the blanket assertion that joining a fraternity or sorority tends to bring lower grades. And it is true that, on some campuses and with some fraternities, members tend to have higher GPAs than the general nonmember population. On *most* campuses, however, Greek letter organization students perform similarly to nonmembers, neither better nor worse.

Fraternities and sororities are most defensive, understandably enough, about the issues of drinking and hazing, pointing out that many Greek letter organizations offer alcohol-free housing or have strict regulations on the use of alcohol. They also generally disavow hazing.

Disclaimers to the contrary notwithstanding, *national* studies have shown a strong link between Greek membership and binge drinking (as well as other substance abuse). But it's certainly true that no fraternity officially requires drinking, and it's possible to find some that actually prohibit it or that make it easy to opt into "dry" housing. National studies have indicated that *many students* join fraternities because they want to drink; nevertheless, *you* don't have to join for that reason.

Despite the findings of national studies, values and standards of behavior vary widely among Greek letter societies and their campuses. This goes for hazing as well, which we'll consider at length in a moment.

Rushing and Pledging

"Rush" and "rushing" refer to the fraternity and sorority recruitment process. Ideally, this process is a two-way street, which gives the organization an opportunity to evaluate prospective members even as it gives those prospects an opportunity to judge the organization.

Whatever else appeals to you about a particular organization—its prestige on campus, the makeup and interests of its members, academic and career networking prospects—use the rush process as a chance to look at the shared values of a group with which you are thinking of associating and identifying:

- Talk to a lot of current members.

- Consider who else is thinking of joining. Are they people you like and respect?

- Ask about values, ethics, and aspects of behavior that are important to you.

- Get GPA statistics for the organization.

- Inspect the housing situation.

Safe Move

Think of rush as an opportunity for you to judge whether or not a particular fraternity or sorority is good enough for you to join.

- ◆ Ask around. Assess the organization's reputation.

- ◆ After the rush process, do a gut check. How do you really feel about these people and this organization?

Following the rush process, active members of a fraternity or sorority meet for a "bid session," in which each person who has expressed interest in pledging the organization is discussed. If the organization decides to invite a "rushee" to pledge (often called "offering a bid"), an invitation goes out. If the invitation—or "bid"—is accepted, the rushee becomes a pledge.

What happens next varies from organization to organization and campus to campus, but all fraternities and sororities lay claim to a certain exclusivity by which members are distinguished from nonmembers. Part of this exclusivity is enforced by an initiation, which typically involves some sort of ritual. In the past, initiation almost invariably involved some kind of painful or embarrassing ordeal—that is, the initiation ritual consisted of hazing.

Hazing

These days, many—but certainly not all—Greek letter organizations specifically disavow "hazing," a term that requires quotation marks because there is no general agreement on what it precisely means. Definitions vary from organization to organization and campus to campus. Forty-three states have laws against hazing (as of summer 2007, the Arizona legislature was considering one, which would make it the forty-fourth state), but even the legal definitions of what constitutes the practice vary. StopHazing.org, a clearinghouse for hazing information and resources, defines it as "any activity expected of someone joining a group (or to maintain full status in a group) that humiliates, degrades or risks emotional and/or physical harm, regardless of the person's willingness to participate."

Let's say a certain initiation ritual is proposed to you. If the previous definition is not sufficient to help you decide whether or not to perform the ritual, StopHazing.org suggests that you ask yourself the following six questions:

1. Is alcohol involved?

2. Will active/current members of the group refuse to participate with the new members and do exactly what they're being asked to do?

3. Does the activity risk emotional or physical abuse?

4. Is there risk of injury or a question of safety?

5. Do you have any reservation describing the activity to your parents, a professor or university official?

6. Would you object to the activity being photographed for the school newspaper or filmed by the local TV news crew?

If the answer to *any* of the questions is yes, you are being hazed.

Little Black Book

Journalism professor and hazing researcher Hank Nuwer has written the definitive study of the dark side of Greek life: *Wrongs of Passage: Fraternities, Sororities, Hazing, and Binge Drinking* (Indiana University Press, 2002). He has also edited a collection of hazing accounts and essays in *The Hazing Reader* (Indiana University Press, 2004). StopHazing.org is an excellent informational website on hazing, not only in Greek letter societies, but in other campus groups.

Some students, parents, and even educators defend hazing as the playing of innocent pranks associated with fraternity initiation. In his book *Wrongs of Passage*, Hank Nuwer pointed out that 35 deaths were attributed to hazing activities between 1838 and 1969. Between 1970 and 1979, 31 students died as a result of hazing and related activities. Between 1980 and 1989, the number rose to 55, and, during the 1990s, 95 hazing-related deaths were reported. Between 2000 and 2001, 29 hazing deaths were reported. Consider: during the 1980s, there were 5.5 college campus deaths annually attributed to hazing. In the year 2000 alone, there were 18 such deaths. Innocent pranks?

Perhaps you still insist that most hazing is just a means to an end. You endure a little pain, a little embarrassment, but you get to join a group of really great people. Before you subscribe to this rationale, consider that, ethically speaking, means can never be separated from ends. Values and behavior are either ethical or they are not. How "great" is a person who teases, tortures, and makes fun of you?

Hazing Examples

Most fraternity and sorority hazing involves the consumption of alcohol, either among those administering the hazing or those being hazed. Many hazing activities are entirely centered on alcohol, typically with the pledge being required to chug large amounts of beer or hard liquor, even highly toxic grain spirits. Most hazing-related deaths result from acute alcohol poisoning, which is discussed in "Substance Abuse," a little later in this chapter.

> **Hard Fact**
>
> Proof is the alcoholic content of beer, wine, or a spirit (such as vodka, tequila, rum, gin, or whiskey). It is determined by multiplying the percentage of alcoholic content by 2, so that, for example, 80-proof vodka contains 40 percent alcohol.

Other examples of common hazing activities include …

- **Spanking.** This is mainly administered in the form of paddling among fraternities, sororities, and other organizations. Sometimes the pledge/victim is put over a lap, a knee, furniture, or a pile of pillows, but more typically the victim is simply ordered to "assume the position": to bend over.

- **Hosing.** The pledge/victim is sprayed down with a garden hose or is doused with buckets of water.

- **Sliming.** The pledge/victim is covered with dirt or food such as eggs, tomatoes, and flour. Sometimes he or she is covered with rotten food.

- **Urination.** Those administering the hazing take turns urinating on the pledge/victim.

- **Tedious cleaning.** The pledge/victim becomes the temporary "slave" of those administering the initiation and is compelled to do chores ranging from ordinary cleaning to such activities as scrubbing a floor with a toothbrush.

♦ **Slavelike behavior.** Current fraternity or sorority members may demand slavelike veneration from pledges/victims, including prostration, kneeling, groveling, foot licking, foot washing, and the like.

♦ **Degradation.** The pledge/victim may be confined in a cage or a barrel, may be commanded to crawl or to walk on all fours, or may be forced to perform other humiliating or degrading acts.

♦ **Forced consumption.** In addition to the binge-drinking activities already mentioned, a pledge/victim may be force-fed raw eggs, peppers, hot sauce, laxatives, insects, rotting food, vomit, or urine. Somewhat more benign versions of this form of hazing include having to eat from "funny" containers, such as a Frisbee or a dog bowl.

♦ **Wearing bizarre or embarrassing clothing.** Examples include having to wear a leash or dog collar, diapers, underwear of the opposite sex (panties for men, men's briefs for women), items of cross-dressing, a condom stretched around the head, fake breasts, and so on.

♦ **Parading naked.** Sometimes complete nudity is required; sometimes the pledge/victim is forced to wear only an apron, a jockstrap, a thong, a necktie, and so on.

♦ **Branding.** The pledge/victim is made to wear symbols, drawings, or text—often obscene or inviting some form of abuse—either on his or her clothing or even on bare skin. Usually, these are painted or inked on, but actual tattooing has been reported and, in a few cases, even hot-iron branding.

♦ **Performing physical feats.** A pledge/victim is required to perform vigorous calisthenics, do push-ups (often with the hazer's foot on his back), engage in mud wrestling, form a human pyramid, climb a greased pole, or perform any number of other difficult tasks.

♦ **Exposure to the elements.** Hazing may consist of being forced to run naked, swim, or dive in freezing weather. A pledge/victim may be forced to embrace a bag of ice or sit naked on a pile of ice or snow.

- ◆ **Abandonment.** The pledge/victim is blindfolded, driven to a remote location, then abandoned to find his or her own way back. Sometimes, he or she is tied up before being dumped.

- ◆ **Challenges and dares.** Hazers dare a pledge/victim to bungee jump, to shoplift, to commit an act of vandalism, and so on.

- ◆ **Quizzes.** Most Greek letter organizations—even those that explicitly disavow hazing—require pledges to study material relating to their fraternity or school. Current members then administer exams or pop quizzes. Sometimes the activity does not go beyond this. Often, however, an incorrect answer merits punishment of some sort.

Hazing Myths

Obviously, hazing assumes many forms, and what one person may consider hazing, another may not. Taking into account that there is a range of interpretation, there are some hazing myths that students as well as parents and administrators sometimes use to justify or overlook dangerous and hurtful practices.

The most common myth is that hazing is usually nothing more than a foolish but essentially innocent prank that somehow goes awry. The fact is that hazing is the forcible assertion of power and control over others. It is victimization, that is, premeditated abuse, which is inherently degrading and may be life-threatening.

Another myth is the belief that, in the absence of malicious intent, there is nothing wrong with "a little hazing." But the fact is that even if there is no malicious intention, hazing can still be physically risky and emotionally damaging.

Many students and even some educators and parents believe that hazing can actually be an effective way to teach respect and develop discipline. The problem with this point of view is that respect is not something that is imposed, extorted, or even taught. It is an attitude that is earned. Does a victim of hazing actually learn to *respect* those who hazed him or her? Not likely. Victimization produces no positive attitudes or emotions.

Finally, many insist that if the proposed initiation activity is consensual—the pledge agreeing to the activity—it cannot be deemed hazing. Nevertheless, although state laws concerning hazing vary widely, not one of the 43 states that currently have legislation against hazing admit the victim's consent as a defense in a civil suit. It is a principle of law that even if someone agrees to participate in a potentially hazardous action, his or her apparent consent may not be true consent because of the influence of peer pressure and coercion.

Think You're Immune?

Hazing is a problem in many fraternities and sororities, but it is by no means confined to them. Think you're immune from hazing because you don't belong to a Greek letter organization and have no intention of joining? Think again. Hazing incidents are frequently documented in other areas of campus life, including military organizations, athletic teams, marching bands, "school spirit" groups, religious cults, and certain campus clubs. Learn to recognize hazing and make your decisions about participation accordingly.

Hard Fact
Assuming Arizona's pending legislation will be signed into law by the governor, only Alaska, Montana, South Dakota, Hawaii, New Mexico, and Wyoming do not have specific laws against hazing.

Substance Abuse

As Jeffrey DeSimone reported in his 2006 study "Fraternity Membership and Binge Drinking," mentioned earlier in this chapter, both anecdotal and objective data confirm that "fraternity members drink more heavily than do non-members," and the rate of binge drinking (consuming at least five alcoholic beverages within a few hours, at least once in the past month) is significantly greater among fraternity members than among all college students (69 percent versus 42 percent).

Despite the data, advocates of Greek letter organizations often insist that fraternities do not "cause" alcohol and substance abuse. Expressed in this narrow way—that membership does not *cause* the abuse—the assertion is probably true. Recent studies have shown that fraternity and sorority members had elevated rates of alcohol consumption and substance abuse *before* they joined the organization. The conclusion such studies draw from this data is that a big appetite for booze is one of the factors that influences a student's choice to pledge a Greek letter society to begin with. That is, a student who already abuses alcohol and drugs tends to see Greek life as congenial to such practices. It's likely that such students would socialize together even if fraternities and sororities did not exist—but they do exist.

Binge-Drinking Dangers

Alcohol has been a part of civilized life—well, certainly as long as there has been civilized life. Recently, a number of medical studies have even suggested that, in moderation, alcohol consumption actually has certain health benefits, including stress reduction and improved heart health. No one, however, advocates such activities as drinking (even moderately) and driving, and, certainly no one suggests that binge drinking is a good idea. It is dangerous, and it can prove fatal—either indirectly, as a contributing cause to accidents, or directly, as an acute form of poisoning.

Let us accept the definition of binge drinking as the consumption of five or more alcoholic drinks, including beer, in a row on any one occasion. Based on this definition, 42 percent of all college students and 69 percent of Greek letter organization members engage in this practice. This is an alarming piece of information, because people who binge on a regular basis expose themselves to the following dangers:

- Death or injury due to falls, fires, drowning, or automobile accidents

- Pregnancy or sexually transmitted diseases due to unintended sexual activity

- Becoming the victim—or perpetrator—of date rape or other assault

- Rapid death from alcohol poisoning

Hard Fact

A recent report by the National Institute on Alcohol Abuse and Alcoholism (NIAAA), notes the disturbing consequences of drinking on campus each year: 1,700 college student deaths from alcohol-related causes; 599,000 unintentional injuries; and 97,000 cases of sexual assault and acquaintance rape. (Go to www.collegedrinkingprevention. gov/StatsSummaries/snapshot.aspx for details.)

For most of us, a drink or two removes inhibitions and therefore makes us feel good—high, buzzed, even energized. Yet the fact is that alcohol is a depressant. Consumed in moderation, its effects can be pleasant and harmless (unless you get behind the wheel), but when a large amount is consumed in a short period of time, your body cannot metabolize the alcohol quickly enough, resulting in the rapid accumulation of a high blood alcohol content (BAC).

Now, in most states, a BAC of more than .10 percent means that you are legally drunk (some states put this limit much lower). That's bad enough if you are caught behind the wheel. But binge drinking results in a BAC that is much greater than .10 percent. The rapid and voluminous consumption of alcohol can bring on loss of consciousness and even respiratory arrest. Since you've got to breathe to live, that is very bad news. But even if you don't manage to down enough alcohol to stop your breathing, you may become unconscious, vomit, and choke on your vomit. (In fact, if someone you know has consumed a lot of alcohol or looks like he or she may pass out, do not leave the person alone. Seek medical attention immediately by calling 911 or campus security if you are with anyone who loses consciousness after drinking. Be sure to follow any instructions you are given and carefully monitor the person's breathing until help arrives.)

Even if you don't drink enough to poison yourself, do you really want to be around a bunch of sloppy, puking drunks?

Paying the Piper

Drinking to excess often means more than a nasty hangover in the morning. It has a damaging impact on health, safety, and academic performance—and not only for heavy drinkers, but for the entire campus and even the surrounding community.

The Core Institute (a research organization serving alcohol and drug prevention programs nationally) recently reported that approximately 50 percent of students living in a fraternity or sorority house performed poorly on a test or project, versus about 25 percent of all students. Approximately 70 percent missed a class, versus about 33 percent of all students. In addition, roughly 59 percent had an argument or fight, compared with 35 percent of all students. All of these problems were related to excessive drinking.

Little Black Book

If you think you drink too much—or if you just want to learn more about binge drinking and problem drinking—here are two first-stop resources:

◆ Al-Anon/Alateen. www.al-anon.alateen.org; 1-888-4AL-ANON

◆ National Clearinghouse for Alcohol and Drug Information. http://ncadi.samhsa.gov; 1-800-729-6686

The 2001 Harvard School of Public Health College Alcohol Study found that 83 percent of the residents in a fraternity or sorority house experienced "negative consequences" as a result of other members' drinking. These consequences included serious arguments, assaults, property damage, the burden of having to take care of a drunken student, interrupted study or sleep, unwanted sexual advances, and even sexual assault and acquaintance or "date" rape.

Drug Abuse

In March 2007, the National Center on Addiction and Substance Abuse at Columbia University (CASA) published *Wasting the Best and the Brightest: Substance Abuse at America's Colleges and Universities.* The study found that fraternity and sorority members were more likely to be current marijuana users (21.1 percent vs. 16.4 percent among nonmembers), cocaine users (3.1 percent vs. 1.5 percent), and smokers (25.8 percent vs. 20.7 percent). Fraternity and sorority members were also twice as likely as nonmembers to abuse prescription stimulants such as Adderall, Ritalin, and Dexedrine.

The dangers of substance abuse are discussed in detail in Chapter 8, but we need to note here that abuse is higher among members of Greek letter organizations than nonmembers.

Sexual Assault and Rape

Recently, a National College Women Sexual Victimization (NCWSV) study found that 20 to 25 percent of college women become victims of attempted or completed rape during their college careers. In 90 percent of these cases, the victims knew the perpetrators. In another recent study, 24 percent of sorority women reported having experienced an attempted rape and 17 percent were victims of a completed rape. About half of the attempted and completed rapes occurred in a fraternity house. Other studies have concluded that men in fraternities tend to engage in more nonphysical coercion and use of drugs and alcohol as a sexual strategy than nonmembers.

On a great many campuses, Greek letter organizations have recognized that problems exist with acquaintance, or date, rape and other forms of sexual assault and sexual intimidation, and they have voluntarily introduced awareness and sensitivity training in sexual behavior.

In recent years, an especially bizarre form of sexual exploitation has been associated with some fraternities. Women attending fraternity-sponsored parties have sometimes been encouraged to drink to excess and then, while intoxicated or even semiconscious or entirely unconscious, they have been photographed or videotaped in sexually compromising, exploitive, and embarrassing situations. The photographs and videos have sometimes been published on the Internet, often reaching an audience far beyond the campus.

No fraternity or sorority condones sexual exploitation, sexual assault, or rape, but the fact is that group behavior, especially when it is fueled by alcohol and drugs, can quickly get out of control.

Animal House Meets the Rule of Law

University and college administrations have always had the authority to fine, suspend, or revoke the charter of a fraternity or sorority whose members repeatedly violate school rules or the law. Until recently, Greek letter organizations had little to fear beyond this. Criminal and civil liability were generally deemed to be the burden of the individual, not the organization with which the individual happened to be associated. More recently, however, fraternities and sororities have been held liable in some civil judgments for mishaps occurring on the property of the organization or under the organization's auspices. This has been especially true in cases involving excessive alcohol consumption at organization-sponsored events. Indeed, during the late 1990s, some 20 of the nation's largest Greek organizations banded together to create the National Fraternity Insurance Purchasing Group. In exchange for relatively low group rates, member organizations agree to adhere to strict risk-management policies, which include no kegs and no open parties. Understandably, in view of such restrictions, many organizations have chosen not to join the group.

Holding a fraternity or sorority liable for the behavior of individual members is a controversial legal tactic, which nevertheless is being used with increasing frequency. But individual students and their parents are making a grave error if they count on passing the buck of legal responsibility to a Greek letter society. Regardless of the circumstances and context in which a crime, alcohol-related mishap, drug arrest, hazing injury or death, sexual assault, or vandalism is committed, it is the individual or individuals involved who will be held accountable, even if the organization is compelled to bear some part of the liability.

Peer pressure and group norms and expectations may help explain instances of misbehavior, criminal conduct, and "accidents," but they do not excuse them—especially in the minds of judges and juries.

Intelligently and responsibly conducted, the Greek system offers members social, academic, vocational, and professional benefits, but it can also present an environment that facilitates dangerous behavior that can ruin a night, a semester, a college career, or a life—and maybe more lives than one.

The Least You Need to Know

- ◆ While membership in a fraternity or sorority has benefits, it can also reinforce bad behavior, including binge drinking, drug use, sexual misconduct, and assault in the form of hazing.

- ◆ Many studies show that alcohol and drug use are significantly higher among fraternity/sorority members than among nonmembers.

- ◆ Hazing is associated with many Greek letter societies.

- ◆ About half of attempted and completed rapes on campus occur in fraternity settings.

- ◆ Group norms and peer pressure do not provide a legal or moral excuse for individual behavior. We are all accountable for our own actions.

5

Private Property

In This Chapter

- How *not* to invite a thief
- Locking up
- When to share and when to be selfish
- Holding on to your cash—and your identity
- Inventorying and identifying your property
- About insurance

Most colleges and universities pride themselves on being open places that invite free inquiry and the exchange of ideas. But even in the liberal atmosphere of campus, you want to keep your own stuff. When a paper is due, you want your laptop. When you walk into calculus class, you want that pricey graphing calculator you bought. When it's time to unwind, it's good to know your iPod is where you left it. The open campus and the communal dorm notwithstanding, some things are yours and yours alone, and that's the way you want to keep it.

The problem is that your folks aren't there to protect your things, and the school principal isn't going to swoop down on little Johnny with a demand that he give Susie back her pencil sharpener and erasers. It may not always look that way, but campus living is adult living. There are people to guide and support you, but mostly you're on your own. You have to be aware that the way some people see the world, property exists to be stolen. It's up to you to take charge of your belongings and do all you can to prevent your property from falling prey to a thief's vision of reality.

In Plain Sight

You've just walked into your room—not your dorm room, but your room at home. You've been carrying your iPod and the graphing calculator you recently purchased for more than a hundred dollars. You don't need them at the moment, so you put them down. Do you hide them in a locked drawer? Or do you just set them down on your desk?

Unless you have a nosy brother or sister or live with a kleptomaniac uncle, chances are you set these valuable items on your desk. That they are in plain view is a convenience for you—you'll know where to find them when you need them—and not much of a risk, unless your desk happens to be directly under a first-floor window. Assuming that these items are not on exhibit for any passersby to see, they are probably safe. Your mother or father isn't going to walk off with them, and you have a good deal of control over who you allow into your room.

Unfortunately, the rules that serve you well at home don't apply in the dorm. It *is* your room, but you have less control over it. Leave something in plain sight, and you are inviting a thief.

Hard Fact

Here are the statistics of a large state university (30,000 students) covering theft for a recent year: 63 burglaries were reported to campus police in residence halls. It was impossible, of course, to count nonreported burglaries.

The most effective step you can take to keep your iPod, bells-and-whistles calculator, laptop computer, backpack, or purse from being stolen is to keep them with you or keep them locked up, out of sight. True, they are your property, and you have a right to set your property down on your desk, turn your back, go out the door, then return in the expectation that your property will be right there, waiting for you where you left it. That is your right. But it's also an invitation to theft, because a thief, by definition, doesn't care about your rights.

My Roommate's No Thief!

You know and trust your roommate, and he's not a thief. He's a college student, like you.

But what does it take to be a thief? The only qualification is that you steal something. Theft need not be your career. Steal something, and—poof!—you're a thief. No diploma, license, or membership certificate is required.

Don't offer your roommate or anyone else the opportunity to be a thief. Put your most valuable and most portable stuff away. Lock it up.

A Thief Is Made, Not Born

Many of us enjoy seeing movies or reading stories about master thieves—men or women who can steal anything, no matter how well protected. They can pick any lock, crack any safe, defeat any alarm system, penetrate any barrier, elude any human guard, pass under or over any video surveillance system. Pure Hollywood fantasy? Not at all. Show some people a house protected by a 10-foot wall, and they will show you their 11-foot ladder. A thief with sufficient skill and determination will devise a way to steal almost anything.

Safe Move

You and your roommate(s) are not the only people who go in and out of your room. College maintenance personnel may enter, as well as casual visitors. Any of them could be a thief, if you invite them to be. So even if you welcome someone into your room, don't invite that person to steal. Try to ensure that maintenance and other personnel enter only when you are present. At other times, lock up all of your valuables.

But most thieves are neither very skilled nor very determined. The relatively few who are true pros won't waste time on your iPod. They will case a jewelry store or the equivalent. The vast majority of thieves are opportunists rather than professionals. They snatch whatever is there for the taking. And on a typical day on a typical college campus, students—and others—offer plenty *in plain sight* for the taking.

Don't Be a Victim

You've had a hard day. You walk into your dorm room, and you gratefully shed the day's burdens—including your backpack (which you put on the floor next to your desk chair), your wallet, your checkbook, and your cell phone (all of which you lay on top of your desk). No sooner do you sit yourself on the edge of your bed than a guy from down the hall opens your unlocked door and sticks his head in. "We got pizza. Want some?" No need to ask you twice. You follow your friend down the hall, leaving behind—in plain sight on your desk, door unlocked—a surprisingly big chunk of your life.

Few targets are more inviting to thieves—professional or opportunistic—than an amply stuffed backpack, juicy wallet, fresh checkbook, and tidy cell phone. These are gold mines of cash, credit cards, personal information, and other items of value.

Roommates or suitemates quickly become accustomed to leaving even the most valuable personal items—wallets and checkbooks included—in the common areas of the room or suite. Maybe you really do trust your roommates as you trust your own family, but do you—or *should* you—trust *their* visiting friends and *their* visiting family members?

You won't insult your roommates if you keep your personal stuff secure and away from prying or straying eyes and covetous thoughts. It's always easier to keep things in your possession than to try to get them back.

The bottom line: don't expose yourself. It is right and proper for many things in life to be private, for your eyes only, and completely under your control.

Bad Idea!

Don't allow personal items—including wallets, checkbooks, and anything else containing vital information—to slip out of your control, even for a moment or two. Most people assume that identity theft is a high-tech crime committed by savvy computer hackers. Actually, most identity theft begins with a stolen credit card, driver's license, ID card, or checkbook.

In Class and on Campus

Outside of your dorm room, the plain-sight doctrine applies even more strongly than it does inside.

You are in the cafeteria, purse over your shoulder, loaded-down tray in both hands. You set down the tray on a table and put your purse beside it. *Gotta grab some ketchup.* The condiment bar is just 10 steps away. You leave your tray and purse on the table. When you return, the food is still warm, but the purse is gone.

A beautiful day. You've got 15 minutes until your next class. You really should review the material in Chapter 6. You sit down on a bench under a tree beside the pleasant stream that meanders through campus, you unzip your backpack, fish out the book you need, put the unzipped backpack next to you, bury yourself in Chapter 6, close the book, and slip it back into the backpack. But hold on. Something's wrong. There's too much room in the backpack. Maybe that's because your laptop computer is no longer inside it.

It was a hard quiz, and calculus is far from your favorite subject. You want to get out of class and into the fresh air as soon as humanly possible. You gather up your stuff, get up, and bolt out the door. Halfway down the hall, it hits you. You left your graphing calculator on the desk. You double-time it back to the room. The desktop is clean as a whistle.

You get in your car and drive downtown to a movie. You certainly don't need to bring your backpack into the show, so, instead of taking the time to stash it in the trunk, you just toss it onto the backseat. Two hours later, with the taste of synthetic butter-flavored popcorn still in your mouth, you get that sinking feeling only the sight of a freshly shattered car window can give. Were you the victim of a career criminal or a casual smash-and-grab thief? Does it matter?

It's outrageous and immoral to blame the victim for the crime committed against him or her, but the truth is that most of the time theft wouldn't happen if the victim did not extend an open invitation by leaving something good and valuable in plain sight.

Watch Those Books!

Oddly enough, expensive as they probably are, you may not think of your textbooks as valuable property. After all, who in their right mind would steal *Modern French Grammar* or *Invertebrate Zoology?* But think about it. At the end of the semester, you may keep some of your books for future reference, but chances are, you'll sell a good many of them back to the campus bookstore. The fact is, on campus, it's very easy to turn a book into cash. And what's easy for you is just as easy for a thief.

Securing Your Stuff

Not everything you own is superportable. Your desktop computer, the 20-inch LCD TV in the dorm room, the minifridge—you can't lock these in a drawer, and you can't carry them around with you, either, at least not without looking very weird and getting very weary. Nevertheless, there is a way to keep such items quite secure, and it's a measure you've almost certainly practiced a lot at home.

It's called locking your door.

As discussed in Chapter 3, this is the simplest safety measure of all, and it's truly amazing how well it works. Sure, just about any door can be broken down and any lock defeated. If a thief is determined to break into a vault, chances are he's going to take the time and effort to get himself in. Why? Because he has reason to believe that the payday inside is huge. Now, no offense, but just how much is a thief going to get out of your dorm room? Almost certainly not enough to make it worth the time and risk of getting himself through a locked door. Moreover, while a thief may be able to spend time after hours cracking a bank vault, he's not likely to want to attract attention hanging around outside your locked dorm door at *any* time.

So lock your door, and almost any thief will move on to the next door, and he will keep moving, trying door after door, until he finds one that's unlocked.

This is lucky for you. Lucky for the thief, however, is the fact that, in the typical residence hall, he won't have to try very many doors before he finds one that's unlocked.

Students have a knack for getting very comfortable and very careless very quickly. A residence hall floor can get to seem like one big commune in which everybody trusts everybody else. It's a wonderful feeling—until the TVs, computers, and book bags start sprouting legs and walking off.

Locking your door won't kill the communal buzz. It will just make everyone safer.

A Lock Is Only as Good as Its Key

All dorm-room doors should be equipped with modern locks in good working order. All public doors and windows throughout the residence hall should be equipped with high-quality locking mechanisms. If anything goes wrong with the lock on your door—or if you notice a problem with the locks on any door or window in your residence hall—report the matter to your RA, to building maintenance, and to the campus police. It should be repaired immediately.

Make sure you have a working set of keys. Do not make copies of your keys. Do not give copies to anyone. If you lose a key, report it to building maintenance immediately. The lock on your dormitory door should be changed.

By far the best key system for residence halls is an electronic card access system—the kind most hotels use. With these systems, each new incoming resident gets a new electronic combination. All the old keys floating around are rendered useless. Even better, if you lose a key card or one is stolen, the electronic combination can be changed instantly—a measure that protects everyone.

> **Safe Move**
>
> If you notice a lock or locking mechanism in your residence hall that appears to have been deliberately damaged—that is, shows evidence of tampering—call the campus police immediately. Assume that someone is trying to break in or has already broken in.

Even More to Lock Up

Locking your door is both the easiest and single most important step you can take to make you and your stuff safe. Now, take the next step by locking everything else that can be locked: your desk drawer and your windows—especially if you are on a first or second floor. Make sure that the locks on external doors, to your floor and to the residence hall building, not only function but have not been deliberately defeated. These doors should never be propped open as a "courtesy" to others.

Door safety is most often compromised on moving-in and moving-out days. At these times, it is common to keep external doors propped open. With dozens, even hundreds, of residents moving in or out, such measures may be necessary. During these times, therefore, be extra vigilant. Do not leave your stuff unattended while all doors are wide open. Make certain all props and doorstops are removed after moving day is done. Be sure that all self-locking doors are locked.

Common Sense

The safety advice we've been giving here is the commonest of common sense. That means that it sounds easy—and, in fact, it *is* easy—but we also know that common sense is lacking in many people, including (maybe especially) college students.

Safe Move

Lock your door when you leave. And lock your door when you stay. Keep yourself secure by locking your door even when you are in your room. Rest assured that everybody who wants to visit you will have sufficient common sense to knock.

A good way to get in touch with your own store of common sense is to plan for your weakest moment. Plan for the times when you are tired, hungry, rushed, and therefore vulnerable. Set up a secure place in your room, preferably a locked drawer, and make a habit of automatically putting your stuff there. Keep your dorm room key or access card on your body at all times, and use it to let yourself in and out of your room. Don't give it to anyone else. Where you go, it goes.

Getting Personal

You may be used to sharing everything about yourself with your family or close friends in high school. While sharing may make you feel generous and, in some cases, even give you a mildly exciting conspiratorial feeling, it can be dangerous, destructive, and even deadly.

Do not "share" with anyone your access code to any secure location. Predators really do lurk in the shadows, patiently waiting for the opportunity to pounce. They listen. They learn. Tell someone your access code, and, if a bad actor is within earshot, he'll hear it, commit it to memory, and use it. Count on that.

How and When to Be Selfish

Theft is not the only means by which you can lose your stuff. Polonius, the well-meaning father of Ophelia in Shakespeare's *Hamlet*, cautions the Prince of Denmark, "Neither a borrower nor a lender be." As with all advice from people over 30, it is neither to be swallowed whole nor entirely rejected. We all need to borrow some things sometime, and most of us enjoy being helpful and generous whenever possible. Just don't lend anything you cannot replace, anything that would cause major grief if lost, or anything that is illegal to lend.

ID cards, driver's licenses, and the like must never be shared. It is illegal to lend someone your ID or access card for any purpose. Lend your visiting friend your campus access card to get him a discount at the cafeteria, and you may lose your own discount privileges. Lend your underage friend your driver's license so that he can get a drink at the bar, and you may lose your license, go to jail, get slapped with a fine, or suffer some combination of these penalties.

These days, software manufacturers have been introducing all sorts of safeguards to discourage bootlegging and unauthorized use of copyrighted computer programs. Lend a software CD to someone who didn't pay for it, and you may find it unusable when it's returned. The limited license *you* bought may be used up by the freeloading friend you loaned the software to.

Sometimes it's not only okay to be selfish, but downright advisable. Sure, you may feel uncomfortable turning down a friend when he or she asks to borrow your ID, but suck it up: "Sorry, Kate, but I can't risk losing my library borrowing privileges. They check the photo very carefully. Give me a minute, and I'll go to the library with you and check the book out myself."

Risky Business

Every day, we share a lot of information about ourselves. This is often necessary to transact the business we need to transact. But giving up information can be risky, so don't do it unnecessarily.

Never lend anyone your ATM card. Don't trust your keys to anyone else. Don't let anyone use your campus library card or the card allowing you access to the gym or other college facility. Don't try to get a fake ID or use one. Don't let anyone use your personal information to put together any false documents. Never give out PINs and computer passwords to anyone, even close friends.

Be very careful about your checks. We like to think that a personal check is valueless, and therefore perfectly safe, until it's filled out and signed by us. Unfortunately, check fraud schemes abound, and it is all too common for check washing or counterfeiting rings to operate on campuses nationwide.

With your check, a scanner, and a basic computer system, there is no limit to the harm some people can do to your financial well-being. Guard your checks as you do your cash and your credit cards. Use personal checks to pay businesses, utilities, government agencies, or college and university expenses that cannot be paid any other way. Avoid using your personal checking account to pay any individual on campus. There is little reason that you should ever have to pay an individual by check. Also avoid using your personal account to fund any student-run campus activity. You should not give your check to a student treasurer or other organization officer.

Here's a scheme that is being reported with alarming frequency in many college communities: You enter or leave the branch bank near campus, the bank in which you have an account. While you are outside the bank, someone approaches you and asks for your help. She (or he) tells you she has a check, but does not have an account at that bank. The problem is, she needs money right away for some emergency; the nature of the emergency varies, but it is always urgent and compelling. She makes out the check to you, asks you to deposit it into your account, draw out cash, and keep a portion of the deposit amount for your trouble. It seems like a win-win proposition. You get to help someone out, and you make a little money for yourself. As for the check, it certainly looks perfectly legitimate.

Of course, there really is no account behind the check she gave you. It is quite worthless—to you. For her, however, it is a golden scoop with a pile of your cash on it.

If you are ever approached in this manner, the proper response is to say no politely, walk away, then call 911 on your cell phone and report the encounter.

Be a good Samaritan by channeling your generous impulses into volunteer work on campus or in the community or by making a donation to a trusted organized charity of your choice.

Take Stock

Know what you have. Make a list of your valuables, including model numbers and serial numbers of such items as computers, iPods, portable stereos, TVs, cell phones, calculators, and the like. If any of these are recent purchases, make sure you keep your receipts. It's even a good idea to snap some digital pictures of your more expensive stuff. All of these records will assist you if you need to file an insurance claim, make a stolen property report to the police, or claim property that the police recover.

Is all this a lot of work? Well, yes—and the more stuff you bring with you to campus, the more work it is. Going off to college is a good time to pare down, to decide what things are really important to you and what things you can leave behind. It's not the time for a display of conspicuous consumption. Bling is not cool on campus. Loading yourself down with expensive stuff may make you the envy of some, but it will also paint you as a target for those who mean you no good. Besides, everything you drag with you to college will have to be dragged back home again at the end of the semester.

Plan to get by with just what you need and no more. If in doubt, leave it behind. You can always ask Mom or Dad to bring something to you later.

Make Your Mark

Put your name on everything you own. Use a permanent marker or a laundry marker to identify such items as jackets, book bags, and backpacks. Engraving is a reliable method for identifying computer and other electronic equipment. Engraving pens can be purchased inexpensively, or you may be able to borrow an engraver from your hometown neighborhood police station or from campus police. Alternatively, you can use an ultraviolet (UV) pen, which leaves an invisible mark on items that can only be seen under a UV lamp. This means you don't need to deface your property, but it also reduces the deterrent value of identification. A thief can't see your mark.

Bad Idea!

Some police and neighborhood watch organizations advise marking property with your Social Security number or license number. But it seems to us a very bad idea to give a thief such personal ID information. Just use your name and nothing else—not your Social Security number, address, or telephone number.

Putting your mark on your stuff is not only a good security move, it also avoids disputes with roommates when it comes time to move. Your graphing calculator may be identical to his—except for your name on it. Just don't take identification to unreasonable extremes. You should expect and tolerate some unwanted sharing of food left in a refrigerator, and if your roommate borrows your pen to jot down an address, so be it.

Insurance Matters

The takeaway message of this chapter is that there are any number of people out there who want your stuff and your money, too. Make it hard for others to steal from you, and you will probably hang on to both.

Not that there are any guarantees, and that's why insurance is one of America's biggest industries. The good news is that, if you live in a dorm, chances are that your belongings are covered under your parents' homeowner's policy. Check on this *before* the college year begins. Be especially careful to take note of any coverage limits that apply to computers, televisions, and stereos. It's a good idea to consult with your parents' insurance agent. If necessary, get special riders to provide any extra coverage you want.

If you discover that you're not covered, or if you live off campus, shop around for a renter's policy. Typically, these are quite inexpensive. Your parents' insurance agent is a good source of advice and information about purchasing an appropriate policy, and your school may also offer a connection to an agent or supplier.

 Bad Idea!

Don't wait until you become a victim of theft to discover that you are not covered by your parents' insurance. The biggest drawback to insurance is this: you have to get it before you need it.

The Least You Need to Know

♦ The vast majority of thieves are opportunists who take whatever happens to be in plain sight. If you put your stuff away, carry it with you, or keep it behind a locked door, it probably will not get stolen.

♦ The most powerful weapon you can point at a thief is a locked door.

♦ Never lend anything that would be difficult, costly, or impossible to replace. Never lend items of personal identification or authorization, such as a driver's license, college ID, or campus access card.

♦ Beware of schemes aimed at gaining access to your financial accounts or your identity.

♦ Make an inventory of your valuables, including model and serial numbers, and make certain that expensive items are covered by insurance.

Chapter 6

Web Life

In This Chapter

- ◆ The Internet. the risks of easy access
- ◆ Social engineering, identity theft, and other scams
- ◆ Staying safe on MySpace, Facebook, and other social websites
- ◆ Don't break the law online
- ◆ Safe dating online
- ◆ Secure shopping online

It's just about impossible to overstate the importance of the Internet in our lives. Something that barely existed 20 years ago is today a fixture of civilization. There's only one way to put it, really. For us, the Internet is a parallel universe. It's a meeting place, a marketplace, a library, a classroom, a bank, a source of news, an instrument of communication, a means of virtual travel, of virtual experience, of infinite amusement. It is a medium through which we do business. In many colleges and universities, it's the way we register for classes, pay our bills, get homework assignments, obtain lecture and lab notes, turn in papers, and generally communicate—with professors, administrators, and other students.

In short, the Internet is *access*, easy and universal, available to all. It is the technology of democracy. The only freedom it does not offer is freedom from risk, from danger, from the potential for victimization.

Hanging Out in Cyberspace

Every town and village in ancient Greece had a place called the *agora*. The word's usually translated as "market," but actually, the agora was much more than that. Yes, you could buy and sell things here, but it was also a place where people met, where public debates were held, and where private discussions took place. The agora was the nexus of the community, the great meeting place and melting pot.

Today, our agora is the Internet. It is our nexus. Our meeting place.

The ancient Greek agora doubtless had its dangers: thieves, pick-pockets, scammers, orators who had some very bad ideas to promote, probably even some hardened criminals. The agora was an open place. That's what made it so great. It's also what made it dangerous—at least to the unwary, the uninformed, the unseeing, the preoccupied.

In its risks and dangers, the modern Internet also resembles the ancient agora.

A Quick Catalog of Common Risks

You are probably well aware of the most common risks of life online:

- ◆ **Viruses.** These malicious computer programs are designed to corrupt or destroy your operating system, programs, or data. In the days before the widespread use of the Internet, viruses usually entered a computer via diskette—on files or programs. Nowadays, they commonly arrive as e-mail attachments, on shared files, or on unauthorized programs, all typically downloaded from the Internet. Once your computer is infected with a virus, it may spread the infection to other computers—potentially many thousands—via the Internet. Often, a virus will propagate itself, sending itself from your computer to all the e-mail addresses in your address book. Then it will likewise invade the e-mail address books on each of those computers, and further multiply, computer by computer, on and on.

◆ **Trojan horses.** These programs are disguised as legitimate, useful programs, which, because they promise some benefit, persuade you to allow them into your computer. Once downloaded, the Trojan horse performs some malicious or destructive action.

◆ **Worms.** These programs seek information on your computer (and on others'), then spread it across networks, often throughout large portions of the Internet. Some worms acquire and disseminate confidential information, such as passwords, Social Security numbers, and the like.

◆ **Spyware and adware.** Often—but not always—less overtly malicious and destructive than viruses, Trojan horses, and worms, spyware and adware are typically downloaded without your knowledge or consent when you surf certain websites. Most of these programs are used by online merchants to monitor your interests and buying habits and to flood you with pop-ups to entice you to buy various products. As such, they are annoying, offensive, and invasive—and they can slow the Internet performance of your computer. Some spyware and adware are downright evil, exposing personal information that can lead to identity theft.

Hard Fact

The term "Trojan horse" comes from the story the Greek poet Homer (circa 850 B.C.E.) tells in his *Iliad* about the fall of Troy. Unable after years of siege to penetrate the walls of the city of Troy, the Greeks pretend to give up, leaving behind a giant wooden horse, just outside the city gates. Persuaded that the Trojan horse is a kind of peace offering or gift, the people of Troy open their gates, roll the thing in, then spend the night partying. While the Trojans sleep off their collective drunken stupor, a small band of Greek warriors emerge from the Trojan horse—which is hollow—and destroy the city from the inside.

All of these hazards can be destructive, wiping out the data (including, say, your semester's notes and coursework) on your hard drive or stealing personal and financial information. Despite their great potential for doing harm, malicious software is today fairly easy to combat using widely available, reasonably priced anti-virus and Internet privacy software.

Fighting Malware and Spam

Viruses and spyware are collectively known as malware. Fortunately, highly effective anti-virus, anti-spyware, anti-spam, and general Internet security software abound. The leading vendors of programs include:

AhnLab, Inc.
V3
ACS
http://info.ahnlab.com/english

Aladdin Knowledge Systems
eSafe
www.aladdin.com/esafe/default.asp

ALWIL Software
avast!
www.avast.com

Authentium, Inc.
Command Antivirus for Windows
www.authentium.com

Computer Associates International, Inc.
eTrust Antivirus
www3.ca.com/Solutions/Product.asp?ID=156

Doctor Web, Ltd.
Dr. Web
www.drweb.com

EScan
www.mwti.net

Eset
NOD32
www.nod32.com/home/home.htm

FRISK Software International
F-Prot Antivirus
www.f-prot.com/products/microsoft

F-Secure Corp.
F-Secure Anti-Virus
www.f-secure.com

Grisoft
AVG Anti-Virus
www.grisoft.com

Kaspersky Lab
Kaspersky Anti-Virus
www.kaspersky.com

McAfee, Inc.
MicroWorld Technologies, Inc.
www.mcafeeb2b.com

Norman
Norman Virus Control (NVC)
www.norman.com/Product/Home_Home_office/Antivirus/en-us

Panda Software
Panda Titanium Antivirus
www.pandasoftware.com/microsoft

Proland Software
Protector Plus
www.protectorplus.com

Sophos
Sophos Anti-Virus
www.sophos.com/products/software/antivirus

Sybari Software, Inc.
Antigen
www.sybari.com/products

Symantec
Many products
www.symantec.com

Trend Micro, Inc.
PC-cillin
www.trendmicro.com

Cyber Scams

More challenging are those threats that exploit the Internet to perpe-
trate swindles and scams, not exclusively with sophisticated malware,
but through *social engineering*.

Social engineering is a cyber-age term for something crooks have been
doing since ... well, ever since crooks have been crooks. Like good old-
fashioned fraud, social engineering uses con-artist trickery to manipulate
people into doing things, spending money, or divulging confidential
information. The difference between the old school and the new is that,
in most cases, the crook never comes face-to-face with the victim. The
whole scheme is worked online.

Corralling the Trojan Horse

Trojan horse software straddles the worlds of malicious computer hack-
ing and social engineering. Online con artists often call Trojan horse
schemes "gimmes." They take advantage of our natural curiosity—or
equally natural greed—to infiltrate the privacy of our computer files.
The Trojan horse gimme typically arrives as an e-mail attachment
promising something for nothing (that is, a "gimme")—maybe a fun free
screen saver, a new free anti-virus or other free system upgrade, a
free can't-miss stock tip—whatever. The keyword and key attraction
is "free." All the recipient has to do is open the e-mail attachment. And
once he or she does that, the Trojan horse is loosed.

Many of today's computer security software suites, as well as features of
recent versions of Microsoft Windows XP and Windows Vista, provide
e-mail filters to help screen out some Trojan horse gimmes; however,
the way to be absolutely safe is to open e-mail attachments only from
sources you absolutely trust—people and companies you know or
from whom you have specifically requested information or a program.
Impulsively surrendering to curiosity or greed can wreak havoc on your
computer files, your bank account, and even your identity.

A variation on the Trojan horse is the "road apple," which, as anyone
who grew up around real-life horses knows, is a synonym for—how
shall we put it?—equine manure. In this case, the social engineer (a.k.a.
crook) leaves a floppy disk, CD, or USB flash drive somewhere he

knows it will be found. The skilled perp ensures that the item looks important, official, and desirable—maybe it is labeled with a college logo and has written on it, "Final Exam questions for History 101." An unsuspecting victim picks the item up, pops it into his computer, and ends up infected. The moral: when you encounter a road apple on your travels, walk around it. Do the same with any diskettes, CDs, DVDs, or flash drives of unknown origin.

Gone Phishin'

Phishing is a highly popular form of social engineering. You receive an e-mail purporting to come from a legitimate source, such as a bank, credit card company, your college bursar's office, even the IRS, requesting "verification" of identity and financial information. Usually, these e-mails carry some dire warning to this or similar effect: "If we do not receive verification of your information within 24 hours, your account will be suspended and your funds unavailable to you." Most of the time, the e-mail contains a hyperlink to a fraudulent but very legitimate-looking web page, complete with official logos and even official content. The page features an authentic-looking fill-in form, which asks you to supply your name, address, phone number, Social Security number, ATM PIN, credit card account numbers, bank account numbers, driver's license, date of birth—in short, your complete identity. And because most of us are so thoroughly conditioned to respond to "official" requests and to fill in "official" forms, we may—without so much as a second thought—cheerfully spill all the beans and then some.

The fact is this: no bank, government agency, university, or other business will ever send you an unsolicited e-mail request for identifying information. Certainly, no legitimate organization will ask for PINs or passwords!

If you receive such an e-mail, take a close look at the address of its source. Most likely, it will be a name without any connection to the purported sender. In any case, if you receive an e-mail asking for personal and financial information, contact—by phone—the company mentioned in the e-mail and report the fraud. Never reply to the e-mail, let alone provide any requested information.

Hard Fact
Some phishing scammers use a phone in addition to a computer. The most sophisticated employ an interactive voice response (IVR) system to counterfeit a very legitimate-sounding version of a bank or other institution's IVR system. The scam works like this: a phony e-mail requests that the victim call a 1-800 number, which the counterfeit IVR answers, requesting the caller to key in account numbers, PINs, and passwords. Some IVR scams even include phony "customer service" representatives, who obtain even more information from callers. How do you fight this scam? Just remember that a legitimate bank or other company will never solicit passwords or PINs from you as a way of "verifying" or "updating" your account.

Social Sites

Malicious software and online scams can be highly destructive. At the very least, they are annoying. All too often, they bring about loss of valuable data or theft of identity—a problem that is usually expensive and time-consuming to fix.

Little Black Book
For an extensive listing of the most popular social websites, check out http://en.wikipedia.org/wiki/List_of_social_networking_websites.

As bad as viruses, Trojan horses, scams, and the like are, there is even worse—maybe far worse.

These days, the Internet offers a large number of "social sites," including MySpace, Facebook, and many others. Such sites offer opportunities to extend your circle of acquaintances deep into cyberspace, and they can be fun, exciting, and useful—a true extension of RL (that's "real life"). As with everything else on the Internet, however, there is a downside—and it is potentially disastrous.

Don't Be Lured

We've all heard horror stories about children who turn up missing or are molested as a result of an online contact. Typically, a predator gets onto a social website, engages a victim in a cyberspace conversation, maybe even swaps webcam images, and eventually "lures"—that is the name of the crime—the victim to a meeting. What happens next can range from molestation, to statutory rape, to sexual assault, to abduction and murder.

Children are among the most vulnerable potential victims of luring (most—but certainly not all—victims of Internet luring are girls 15 years old and older), but anyone, including college students, is potentially at risk.

The rule here is to be extremely wary of making "real-life" contact with people you meet online. If you decide you want to meet, agree on a safe public place and do not go to the meeting alone. Take along a friend or, even better, two friends. Get to know the person IRL ("in real life") before you treat him or her as a friend.

Surf Smart

Abduction, sexual assault, and other forms of physical harm are, of course, the most extreme consequences of the careless use of social websites. More frequently, the damage is a loss of privacy, which can result in annoying commercial exploitation (a sudden and unceasing torrent of spam e-mail, for instance) or costly and destructive criminal identity theft.

You can avoid most of the dangers posed by social websites—yet still use and enjoy them—by remaining as anonymous as possible. Keep personal and financial information to yourself. Give careful thought to how you create an e-mail address or a screen name. The best idea is to use a combination of letters and numbers in e-mail addresses as well as screen names, and avoid names that identify you as male or female.

Bad Idea!

It is always a bad idea to divulge online your full name, home address, phone number, Social Security number, passwords, names of family members, or credit card numbers. If anyone online asks you for these, you can be pretty sure they're up to no good.

When you log onto a chat room, use a nickname that's different from your screen name. This lets you make a quick and clean getaway from a conversation that makes you uncomfortable. You can leave without having to worry that someone can use your screen name to track you down via e-mail. Consider sites that allow you to set up totally private chat rooms—a cozy place for you and your friends, with entrance by invitation only.

Cyberbullying and Threats

The virtual world can be a cold, cruel world. Social websites are sometimes inhabited by cyberbullies, individuals who take perverse pleasure in sending cruel or bullying messages. These range from annoying to frightening to outright threatening.

Unless you feel that you are in personal danger, the most effective response to a cyberbully is to ignore him or her. Whether operating IRL or in virtual reality, most bullies are people looking for attention. Deny them what they are looking for, and they will probably look elsewhere.

It is against the law to threaten, intimidate, or harass anyone online, just as it is to do so in person, on the phone, or via the mail. Don't even think of using a social website—or any other online resource—to threaten or harass anyone. It is illegal, exposing you to criminal charges as well as a civil lawsuit. Plus, it's just plain wrong. If you feel that you have received a serious online threat, contact campus security or the police.

Legal Risks

Anything that is illegal IRL is against the law in cyberspace as well. Larceny—including all the online attacks and scams we've discussed—and making threats are against the law and can lead to criminal and/or civil penalties. Libel—publishing damaging false information about someone—may also get you in trouble. The Internet is a public place, and although the First Amendment to the U.S. Constitution guarantees you free speech, it gives no one immunity from being sued for libel if what you publish on the Internet is malicious, false, and damaging.

The biggest legal risk run by most college-age users of the Internet is illegal file sharing. There are a number of file-sharing networks on the

Internet—some legitimate, some not, all offering such files as movies, songs, and video games. Many, probably most, of these kinds of files are copyrighted by the owner, who, by law, has the right to limit who copies and distributes the material.

You may have heard a lot of confusing talk about file sharing—what's legal and what's not. You may have heard that you're safe as long as all you do is download and not upload—pass on files to others. The facts are actually pretty simple. If you download or upload copyrighted music, movies, software, or anything else without the copyright owner's permission, you are probably violating federal law and exposing yourself—and quite possibly your parents—to lawsuit by the copyright owners.

Another file-sharing danger is infection by virus or other malicious software. Most file sharing is on the peer-to-peer (P2P) model, meaning that the shared files are stored on and uploaded and downloaded from any number of personal computers. Control and oversight are often nonexistent, and individual motives and agendas are anyone's guess. Make sure your computer has a good, up-to-date software security suite onboard.

Safe Move

Only visit file-sharing sites that are legal or use commercial download services. Usually, you have to pay a fee for much of what you download. Movie, recording, and software companies are all cracking down on illegal file sharing. Your actual chances of getting caught may be fairly slim, but these companies have been vigorously pursuing civil suits against those who are caught.

Online Dating

Online dating is really a misnomer. People who visit online dating sites don't really date in cyberspace; instead, they make contact and meet there, get to know a person, then move on to a meeting (and perhaps a bona fide date) in real life. Or not.

Most of the best-known paid online dating sites have a number of safeguards in place, but, as always, safety is first and last your responsibility.

Begin by practicing simple courtesy and honesty. The rules of behavior that apply in real life also apply online. Don't lie about yourself, and if you tell someone you are going to e-mail them, do so.

Little Black Book

The following are the most popular dating websites:

♦ PerfectMatch.com: Attempts a scientific approach to online dating.

♦ eHarmony.com: The focus here is on personality matching.

♦ Match.com: One of the oldest and most widely used dating sites.

Take steps to protect your identity, privacy, and security. Do not provide personal information right away. All a stranger needs is your home phone number and full name to obtain just about every other piece of vital information about you: income and employment data, your home address, and so on. Reputable online dating sites provide you with an e-mail address that is separate from the one you regularly use. If the site does not provide this, sign up for a free Yahoo!, Hotmail, or Gmail account to use exclusively for online dating. Do not put your full name in the e-mail message "From" field; use your first name only or something else. Should you decide to take your communication to the next level—a telephone chat—do not give out your home phone number, your work number, your parents' number, or your dorm phone number. Instead, provide a cell-phone number or an Internet phone service number, such as Skype.

Ask for a recent photograph of the person you are thinking of making a date with. Looks are important—for any number of reasons. Trust your gut instincts. If you do get together with the person, and he or she appears significantly older than the photograph that has been sent to you, cut the date short. At the very least, you're with a liar.

Become well attuned to your e-mail and phone conversations. As you talk, ask yourself: What's this person like? Trust your gut. Danger signals include inappropriate remarks (defined as anything that strikes you as off-color, in bad taste, or that offends you), evidence of a short temper (anger issues), evidence of an overly controlling personality ("We *have* to meet here—and nowhere else"), or evasiveness (avoidance of certain questions).

Use the most popular paid online dating services. They are in business for the long haul and therefore have an investment in their clients' satisfaction and safety. Before you sign up with a site, review its safety policies. On the other hand, do not succumb to the false sense of security some online dating services provide with such claims as subjecting clients to full "background checks." Remember, your safety and security are ultimately your responsibility.

When you decide to meet face to face, always do so in a public place, to which you provide your own round-trip transportation. Do not accept an offer to be picked up at your house or dorm. Be sure to tell a friend—or two—where you are going and who you will be with. Take your cell phone.

Digital Commerce

Is online shopping inherently risky? The answer is a definite yes— and no.

Let's begin with the biggest risk. It is simply this: given the ability to sit in front of your computer or curl up on your bed with your laptop and browse and shop 24 hours out of each of the seven days of the week, there is a very real danger that you will not only max out your credit cards, but that you will do so with alarming speed. Getting into debt— or getting your folks deeper into debt—is no joke. Shop wisely and stay within your means.

Beyond the very real danger of landing in serious hock, most of us fear that putting our credit card information online exposes us to identity and credit card fraud—in other words, becoming the victim of a crime in which someone gets a credit card number and uses it to make a load of unauthorized purchases. Because the Internet is largely anonymous and because most online merchants allow separate billing and shipping addresses, it is relatively easy for a crook to use stolen credit card information. If he pays extra to get overnight shipping—and why wouldn't he, with a stolen account number?—he can get the goods and disappear before any fraud is even discovered.

All of this said, the fact is that your credit card information is no less secure when you put it out onto the Internet by making an online order than when you give someone behind a store counter your credit card. Either way, the data goes out onto the Internet. Moreover, when someone has physical possession of your card, they can copy down account numbers or even swipe the card through a machine that obtains and records account information. On balance, your credit card information may actually be more secure when you deal with reputable online merchants than when you hand your card to someone in a brick-and-mortar store, restaurant, or bar, or when you give out your credit card number over the phone.

Scoping Out a Secure Site

When you walk into a brick-and-mortar store, you can make some judgment as to the merchant's legitimacy. How fancy is the shop? What is the nature and condition of the merchandise? Is the shop part of a familiar chain? But when you log onto a merchant website, you need to know that just about anyone can set up a virtual store and start collecting money. They don't need a well-stocked warehouse. They don't need the backing of a big department-store chain. They don't even need genuine merchandise.

Some of the slickest online crooks have the slickest-looking websites. So how do you tell when you are shopping at a secure site?

Your web browser should be able to handle Secure Socket Layer (SSL), a common encryption method that scrambles private information you send into cyberspace. A majority of reputable e-commerce sites use SSL to transact business with you. If a site does not use SSL, think twice before making a purchase on it. When you use Internet Explorer, look at the top left corner of the screen. When you use Netscape, look to the right of the round "stop" button with the "X" in it. You will find your "browser string," which tells you where you are on the web. Ordinary non-e-commerce sites have browser strings that look like this:

> **Hard Fact**
>
> Both Explorer and Netscape also have another way to indicate that SSL is being used. A padlock icon appears in the bottom right corner of the browser window. If the icon is unlocked, you are not browsing an SSL page; if it is locked in the closed position, you are on an SSL page.

http://www.anysite.com. Sites that use SSL have browser strings like this: https://www.anysite.com/. The "s" after "http" reveals that the site uses SSL.

Be aware that not all pages on an e-commerce website need to be secure with SSL. Only when you actually go to check out—that is, when you go to the page that accepts your credit card information—do you really need to see that SSL indication.

A Question of Identity

It's easy to feel secure when you are dealing with the website of a big, well-known merchant. But what about less familiar merchants? The ones that don't have a big brand name? E-commerce is a great equalizer, a wonderful way for small, specialized merchants, craftspeople, collectors, and the like to get their wares before the public. It would be a shame to pass up a perfectly good guy because you don't know whether to trust him.

You can tell almost nothing from the look of the website. Anyone can appear professional on the Net. What scammers almost never do, however, is provide a real-world street address or even a P.O. box number. All legitimate sites include some form of physical address. Also, you need to see a telephone number. If you are in doubt, use that number to give the merchant a call. A real live person should be on the other end—even if you have to go through an automated system and ultimately press "O" to get to him or her.

 Bad Idea!

Avoid shopping at sites that allow contact by e-mail only—or that provide no means of contact at all. Even if your merchandise is shipped, who are you going to talk to if there's a problem with the stuff?

Seller Reviews

When you buy from such online auction sites as eBay, read the seller reviews. Buy only from sellers with a lot of reviews, the overwhelming proportion of them solidly positive. Avoid sellers with any significant number of negative reviews—and, equally important, sellers with very few or no reviews. As always, if a deal looks too good to be true, it almost certainly is.

Privacy, Please

The site of a reputable online seller always includes a clear statement of its privacy policy, including an explanation of how it uses whatever information it collects about you. Reputable sellers include checkboxes you can click—or unclick—to opt out of any or all mailing lists. If the seller's site does not include a policy statement or permit opting out, think carefully before giving the merchant your business.

Many Happy Returns?

Like their brick-and-mortar brethren, reputable online merchants have a reasonable return policy, which you don't have to look hard to find. They also offer customer service, whether by e-mail or phone—though a phone option is always preferable.

Buyer Beware

We've said it before, and we'll say it again. As with all other aspects of online safety—and, indeed, all issues of safety and security—the first and last responsibility is yours. Veteran computer programmers are fond of the acronym GIGO, which stands for "garbage in, garbage out." Make sure that your communication with the online merchant is clear and accurate. Double-check your order form, especially ensuring that credit card account numbers are correct, shipping and billing addresses are accurate, and quantities, model numbers, and money amounts all check out.

The Least You Need to Know

- ◆ It would be very hard—and a lot less fun—to live without the Internet, but along with all the good things it brings us comes a load of risks, ranging from annoying to catastrophic.

- ◆ Malicious individuals use a variety of software tools as well as social engineering to commit digital vandalism (data corruption and destruction), credit card fraud, identity theft, a variety of scams, and outright predation.

- Social websites such as MySpace and Facebook can expand your circle of acquaintances into cyberspace, but, unless used with prudent caution and vigilance, can expose you to financial and physical harm.

- Copyright infringement through illegal file sharing—including the downloading and uploading of music, videos, games, and the like—can lead to federal criminal prosecution and massive lawsuits from copyright holders.

- Online dating is not inherently dangerous, if you practice common sense and guard your privacy.

- Online shopping is convenient and often offers the best deals—provided that you take the time to be vigilant.

Chapter 7

Out and About

In This Chapter

- ◆ The myth of the ivory tower
- ◆ Staying safe while driving and parking your car
- ◆ Thwarting carjackers
- ◆ Biking and walking safely
- ◆ Security at the ATM
- ◆ Public transit tips

In 2006, the National Safety Council published the odds of dying from a variety of causes (all of them unpleasant, however), based on the most recent year for which detailed data was available, 2003. Violent criminal assault killed 17,732 Americans that year, which translated into a 1 in 16,403 chance that you—and any individual living in America—would be killed in an assault in any given year. Your chances of meeting such a fate during your lifetime were calculated at 1 in 211.

On a day-to-day basis, people tend to be much less concerned about noncriminal "external" causes of injury and death—that is, accidents—than they are about being killed in a criminal assault;

however, the odds of accidental death are generally much more stacked against you. In 2003, 166,857 accidental deaths were recorded in the United States. In any year, your odds of being killed by accident are 1 in 1,743, and your lifetime odds of meeting such an accidental end were calculated as 1 in 22.

The point? Ours is a world with significant risks, and we *worry* about it. This chapter shows you how to *do something* about it.

Ivory Tower?

It used to be fashionable to say that academics—faculty, administrators, and students alike—inhabited an "ivory tower," a place high above the daily fray, insulated and isolated from the often harsh, sometimes violent realities of life outside the "ivy-covered walls." Such horrific events as a spate of high-school killing sprees—the most infamous having occurred at Columbine High School (Littleton, Colorado) in 1999— and the mass murder at Virginia Tech (Blacksburg, Virginia) in 2007 have pretty well shattered the ivory tower illusion.

Or at least they should have—because the ivory tower has always been an illusion, a myth. The college campus and the larger community around the campus are often pleasant, even lovely places, but they are not and never have been immune to crime and accident. In fact, campuses and college communities are subject to the same risks and hazards of any American community.

Although such legislation as the Clery Act (see Chapter 2) and statistics compiled by the U.S. Department of Education's Office of Postsecondary Education make it easy for anyone to get a snapshot of campus and student-related crime, there is no overall national data on accidents among college students, on campus or off. It is probably safe to assume, however, that accident rates are comparable to those for the general population. The takeaway is this:

> **Little Black Book**
>
> For comprehensive statistics on campus and off-campus crime, see http://ope.ed.gov/security/main.asp. The National Safety Council's stats on accidents can be found at www.nsc.org/lrs/statinfo/odds.htm.

1. Campuses are not immune to crime and accident.

2. As generalized statistics, the odds of coming to harm as a result of crime or accident are what they are, but you, as an individual, can significantly reduce the odds that you will become a victim of crime or accident by accepting personal responsibility for vigilance, the practice of common sense, and the acceptance of a little advice.

Defensive Driving Revisited

There was a time when the typical college or university campus was an auto-free oasis, the exclusive domain of pedestrians and bicyclists. Today, some traditional campuses preserve a vehicle-free core, but, for the most part, streets, roads, parking lots, and parking structures are thoroughly integrated into the college experience. At urban campuses, buildings are often sited right on city streets, just like the buildings of any other business or institution. Most of today's college and university campuses are a mix of vehicle and pedestrian traffic.

We're not going to teach you how to drive—you've already been taught—but we do have some advice on defensive driving—driving practices that reduce risk by encouraging you to anticipate dangerous situations, especially the mistakes of others—in an environment loaded with cars and people.

The most obvious advice is this: watch out for walkers. Driving on campus, you not only need to give pedestrians the right of way, you need to give them plenty of extra room. Walking from class to class, student-pedestrians tend to feel entitled. Crossing the street in his hometown, a student looks both ways, but crossing a street on campus, all he wants to do is get to class on time, and he may well feel that it's up to the cars to stop for him.

Whatever else a college campus is, it's a densely populated community. That means not only the presence of a lot of pedestrians, but also a good many cars—whose drivers, more likely than not, are variously preoccupied with talking on cell phones, listening to iPods, looking at the sights, looking for a particular building, or (on many jammed campuses) looking for a place to park. Driving defensively requires anticipating the inattention of other drivers—and compensating for it with your own extra-careful attention.

Before You Start Up

If you have a car on campus, it is up to you to take the time to maintain it for safety. Before you start your car, do the following:

◆ Be sure your tires are in good shape. At least once a month, check tire pressure, tread wear, and general condition. Driving with low tire pressure not only consumes expensive gas, it causes poor handling and may even bring on tire failure—a catastrophic blowout—especially at highway speeds.

◆ Make sure your headlights and all other lights work, and that windows, mirrors, and lamp lenses are clean.

◆ Check oil, fuel, and water levels regularly, and keep your car adequately maintained.

◆ Lock all of your doors as soon as you get into the car. Make this a habit.

◆ Buckle up—and make sure that all passengers are wearing their seatbelts.

◆ Secure all loose objects inside the vehicle. Move anything large into the trunk.

Safe Move

Wearing your seatbelt is the single most effective step you can take to reduce your chances of death or injury in a crash. Insist that all of your passengers buckle up—not just for their own safety, but because, in most places, it is now the law. If you are pulled over for your failure to wear your seatbelt—or for your passengers' failure to do so—*you* will get a ticket, a hefty fine, and points on your license, which may raise your insurance premium.

Check all gauges after you start the engine. Before you start moving, perform a circle check. That means looking all around you. Don't rely on your mirrors. Look directly through the back window. The circle check is especially important in a campus environment with all those pedestrians. If possible, park where you won't have to back up, but can pull out.

On the Move

Before you pull out of a parking space, use your turn signal and check for traffic and pedestrians. This is especially important on busy campus streets, because, on campus, many people walk on the street as well as the sidewalk.

Once you are on the move, practice courtesy to other drivers and pedestrians. It's always safest to drive in a pleasant and generous frame of mind. If you're angry or upset, try to avoid getting behind the wheel. Driving transforms the behavior of many people—and rarely for the better. Bad behavior ranges from rudeness—often manifested in a well-known digital gesture—to outright "road rage," a phrase that describes violent driving behavior. Not only is it your responsibility to avoid road rage yourself, you need to act defensively to avoid provoking it in others. A good rule of thumb is to remember that the right of way is given, never taken. In other words, when in doubt, yield to the other driver.

Make certain that you can see and be seen. Anticipate. Scan the road well ahead. Watch ahead for brake lights and for sudden or urgent vehicle movement, both of which signal a problem to which you will have to react.

Know your brakes. If your vehicle is equipped with antilock brakes, get used to them. With antilock brakes, the brake pedal will vibrate in a hard or panic stop. You will both feel and hear the vibration, which typically feels and sounds as if you are running over a washboard. Your impulse may be to let up on the brake. Do not do this! The vibration is the proper action of the antilock brakes, which are designed to prevent your wheels from locking up, so that you can keep steering effectively, even though you are applying full braking power. Hold your foot down, hard, and let the brakes do their work. Do not pump antilock brakes.

At all intersections—especially when driving on a campus active with pedestrians—keep your wheels straight while you are waiting to turn across oncoming traffic or across a pedestrian walkway. If a distracted driver rear-ends your car, you won't be pushed into the opposite lane or into unsuspecting pedestrians.

On the street and especially on the highway, keep an ample distance between your car and the car ahead. You should be able to stop safely in the visible amount of road ahead. A good rule of thumb is to maintain at least a three-second interval between your car and the one ahead of you. To gauge this, note when the car ahead passes some stationary marker, such as a sign. Count *one-one thousand, two-one thousand, three-one thousand*. If you reach the sign before the third count, you are following too closely and should slow down.

Hard Fact

According to the National Safety Council, in a typical year, you have a 1 in 6,498 chance of being killed in a motor vehicle–related accident. Over your lifetime, the odds jump to 1 in 84. You are better off if you remain a pedestrian, but you are still far from safe. There were 5,991 pedestrian fatalities in 2003, yielding a 1 in 48,458 chance of death in a typical year. Your lifetime chances of being killed as you cross the street or walk along a highway are 1 in 626.

Do not drive in the blind spot of other vehicles, and be sure to use your turn signals well in advance whenever making a turn or lane change. Pace yourself with traffic. Speeding is dangerous, but so is driving much more slowly than everyone else.

In any situation, vigilance is the most important element in staying safe. When you are driving, focus on driving. Do not talk on a cell phone, do not eat, and do not drink. Don't become distracted by other passengers in the car. Just drive.

Assume the Worst in Others

Assuming the worst in others is generally a terrible prescription for living your life, but it is the very foundation of effective defensive driving.

You are at an intersection, about to make a right turn on red. You look to your left and see a car approaching with its right turn signal on. Assuming he does indeed turn, you are free to make your right. But what if he goes straight ahead, through the intersection? What if he is unaware that his turn signal is blinking?

Defensive drivers expect that a vehicle indicating a turn may not, in fact, turn.

They also assume that a given vehicle may suddenly turn without signaling. And they anticipate that stop lights and stop signs will be ignored—and they are ready for anything when they approach an intersection.

People run red lights all the time. Don't be in such a hurry to get off the mark when your light turns green, especially at a crowded intersection.

Watch out for distracted drivers: drivers looking the wrong way at an intersection, drivers on cell phones, drivers who seem confused. Watch out for drunk or impaired drivers. They often drive much too fast or much too slowly, and they tend to drift over lane lines, brake too late at intersections, stop abruptly, or respond slowly to traffic signals. Give these drivers a wide berth.

Look out for visibly damaged or visibly defective cars. Avoid them. Chances are, the damage is a record of the other guy's driving skills— or, more precisely, the lack thereof.

Plan a Way Out and Avoid Danger

Whether driving on the highway or on campus, always look for a way out. Try to keep the space on either side of your car free. On freeways, drive in the outer lane as much as possible to avoid having to cross traffic lanes to get to the breakdown lane. On undivided four-lane highways, 95 percent of fatal collisions occur in the inside lane. Also avoid driving next to large vehicles longer than necessary. Trucks and similar vehicles have significant blind spots, and a turning truck can suddenly cut you off.

Tailgaters can be unnerving. If you are being closely followed, pull over to the right, if possible, and let the other vehicle pass. If you cannot do this, slow down gradually. Usually, the tailgater will back off—and, in any case, you will have extra distance between you and the car in front of you, which will allow distance for both you and the tailgater to stop safely, if necessary.

Look out for objects in the road. If you can do so safely, drive around them—even if they look harmless. A fallen tree branch, for example, can puncture a tire or even the fuel tank.

Parking

Perhaps the most dangerous time for drivers is when they are leaving or entering their cars. If you exit on the traveled side of a street or road, look both ways before you open the door. Remember, too, that you are vulnerable to assault as you enter or exit your car. Be vigilant.

Leaving Your Car

Whether you are on or off campus, whenever possible, park as close to your destination as you can. If you have to, it's worth waiting a few extra minutes for a parking space. When it's dark, try to park under a street light or in another well-lighted area. In a parking lot, consider backing into the space, so that you will be facing forward and can drive away quickly, if you have to.

After you have parked, leave your engine running until you've gathered everything you are taking with you and are ready to exit. Before you open the door, survey your surroundings. Never leave anything within sight in your car. Shopping bags, purses, briefcases, suitcases, laptop cases, music players, articles of clothing, loose change—anything left in a parked car is an invitation to a smash-and-grab break-in. Hide everything, putting large items in the trunk, or take the stuff with you. Once you leave the car, choose the best-lit route from the car to your destination.

Remember that lack of awareness—a lapse in vigilance—is vulnerability. Take responsibility for knowing where you are and what's going on around you. Use positive, self-confident body language. When you get out of your car and start walking, keep your head up, stand straight up, and walk assertively, swinging your arms.

Use common sense about where you park. It may not be possible to get your first choice, but by all means avoid alleys or other secluded spots. Do not purposely put yourself in the wrong place at the wrong time.

Parking Garages

On and off campus, parking garages and other enclosed parking structures abound. Many of these are desolate, dim, and creepy places. They are not necessarily any more dangerous than open parking lots. In fact, because many are staffed and are also furnished with surveillance cameras, they may actually be among the safer places to park. Nevertheless, vigilance and awareness are called for.

When you park in a garage, look around you before exiting. Before you reenter your vehicle, look into it, especially at the passenger side floor and in the backseat. If a big van is parked next to the driver's side, enter your car from the passenger door, if possible. Would-be assailants have been known to attack a victim by pulling her into their van while she attempts to get into her car. (Most—but not all—such attacks are against women.) In fact, this is a good reason to park away from big vans.

It is also a good idea to look at the car parked beside your vehicle. If someone is just sitting in the adjacent car, and if he, she, or they just don't "look right" to you, trust your instincts. If you are pulling in, choose another space. If you are approaching your vehicle to leave the parking garage, walk back to safety, alert an attendant (if one is present), or call the police. At the very least, you can get an escort to your car.

Safe Move

On many campuses, campus security or police will provide escort service on request. Inquire about the availability of this service on your campus—and use it.

In any multilevel parking garage, it is always safer to take the elevator rather than the stairs. Stairwells are mostly invisible to the public. They are choice spots for violent crime. Elevators, on the other hand, usually have surveillance cameras. However, don't get on the elevator if you are made uncomfortable by somebody who is already in it or waiting for it. Once you are in the elevator, avoid standing in the corner. Position yourself up front, near the door, ready to leave. If someone suspicious gets on—get off, regardless of what floor you're at. Trust your instincts. Sacrifice convenience for safety.

Returning to Your Car

Whether you are parked in a garage, lot, or on the street, when you are returning to your car, have your keys in hand, ready to open the door, so that you can get in quickly. A key firmly in hand also makes a good weapon, if you are assaulted.

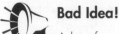

Bad Idea!

A lot of us get into our cars, make a cell phone call, write notes, record an expense in a checkbook, whatever. Don't use your parked car as your office. Make it your business to get inside the vehicle, lock the doors, and leave.

If it is after hours or you are in an unfamiliar place, take the best-lit route to your car and be alert. Survey the area around your vehicle before approaching it. Once you get inside your vehicle, lock the doors.

In Chapter 15, we will talk specifically about self-defense methods, but for now, know that if you are approached by an assailant, call as much attention to yourself as possible by honking your horn and flashing your lights. Of course, if you're inside the car, the best thing to do is to drive away as soon as possible. If you are outside of your car and are approached by a predator with a gun, your best move is to run. It is much harder to hit a moving, fleeing target than a stationary one. Under the stress of a foot pursuit, trained marksmen—such as the police—hit their target with 4 out of 10 shots at a range of 3 to 9 feet. Chances are that a gun-wielding assailant is not a trained marksman and cannot handle stress as effectively as a policeman. Experts estimate that a predator will hit a running target only 4 times in 100—and even then, his shot most likely will not find a vital organ. Run, yell, and get away, fast!

Remember: trust your instincts. If you sense danger as you return to your car, don't ignore the feeling in the hope that it will go away and everything will be okay. Withdraw to a safe place until you are sure that it is safe to proceed. If you are unsure, call campus security or the police. Cops would much rather prevent crime than deal with its aftermath.

Carjacking

On average, between 1993 and 2002—the period for which the fullest statistics have been compiled by the U.S. Department of Justice—38,000 carjackings occurred annually in the United States. The Justice Department defines a carjacking as a completed or attempted robbery of a motor vehicle by a stranger to the victim. Unlike motor vehicle theft, in a carjacking the victim is present and the offender uses or threatens to use force.

Some truths about carjacking, courtesy of the FBI:

♦ Men are more often victimized than women.

♦ Carjacking happens most often in urban areas, followed by suburban and rural areas.

♦ A weapon is used in nearly three quarters (74 percent) of carjackings.

♦ Males commit more than 90 percent of carjackings.

♦ More than two thirds of carjackings occur at night or early morning, between 6 P.M. and 6 A.M.

♦ Forty-four percent of carjacking incidents occurred in an open area, such as on the street, and 24 percent occurred in parking lots or garages.

You can reduce your odds of being carjacked by trying to avoid driving in isolated areas. If you have to take an unfamiliar route or drive in an unfamiliar area, get good directions and make sure you understand them before you set out. Avoid having to pull over to read directions.

As always, be alert to what's happening around you. Avoid tailgating. Not only is this an unsafe—and illegal—driving practice, it plays into the carjacker's favorite tactic. Sometimes working as a two-vehicle team, carjackers box in their target, leaving you no way out. Don't become an accomplice in a crime against you. When you are stopped in traffic, leave enough room between you and the car in front of you to get away. One car length is sufficient.

Carjackers sometimes flash their lights at you and indicate that you should pull over. If you decide to pull over, do so only in a very public place, preferably the parking lot of a convenience-type store or a strip mall. Another option is to use your cell phone to call 911 and report that a motorist signaling you.

It is not uncommon for a carjacker to impersonate a police officer, even using a red or blue flashing light on his vehicle. Do not pull over unless you are certain that the other vehicle is a police car driven by a police officer. If you are in doubt, keep driving, use your cell phone to dial 911 and call the police, advise the 911 operator of your location and situation, and continue to drive to a well-lighted public area, such as a store.

If you are approached while stopped, ensure that all doors are locked, and do not roll down your window more than one inch. Ask to see the badge and identification of anyone who announces himself as a police officer.

If you *are* carjacked, do not resist. Pay attention to what the carjacker tells you. If you are alone, just try to get out of the car and get away. Let the thief have the car.

On Two Wheels

Bikes and scooters are increasingly popular among today's environmentally responsible college students. The idea is to share the road safely with cars and pedestrians. That means obeying all traffic laws and regulations, including stop signs and stoplights. It also means biking on the right and going in the right direction on one-way streets. Always yield to pedestrians.

> **Little Black Book**
>
> A full discussion of bicycle and scooter safety is beyond the scope of this book. For great bicycle safety tips—from bike enthusiasts—go to BicycleSafe.com. The safety manual *You and Your Scooter* is available for free download at http://abacus-es.net/motorscooter/yourscooter.html.

The biggest problem drivers of two-wheel vehicles have is visibility to drivers of four-wheel vehicles. Wear reflective clothing, and make sure your bike is equipped with a rear reflector and a working headlight. Make eye contact with drivers. Be sure they see you.

Walking the Walk

Whether on campus or in the community beyond, college students do a lot of walking. It's a great way to get around, it's healthy, it's fun, and there is no better way to get acquainted with your campus and your community than exploring them on foot. But even if you like to travel light when you're walking, never leave your common sense behind.

True, you and/or your parents pay a lot of money to keep you in college, and that may give you the feeling that you "own" the place. But it is a bad idea to walk around campus as if you have it all to yourself. Don't jaywalk, do pay attention to traffic lights, and, even if you have the right of way, don't assume that oncoming car will stop.

Even if you are just out for a stroll, it is a good idea to have a destination and to plan ahead how you intend to get there. At the very least, don't give the appearance of aimless wandering. Walk as if you have a purpose. Radiate confidence. Use positive body language, including a head held high and posture maintained upright. Swing your arms. This not only makes walking easier, it gives you a look of self-assurance. On a sidewalk, you are safest walking near the curb, which gives you the best view of your route. Buildings and shrubs may screen your view.

Don't glue your eyes to your own two feet. Look up and ahead. Scan the distance. Look around you, and, from time to time, glance behind. Take advantage of reflective surfaces, such as store windows, to check out what's behind you or across from you. Remember, it is your responsibility to be alert.

Dress for walking. Wear comfortable shoes and nonrestrictive clothing. Don't wear flashy jewelry, expensive sneakers, or designer clothing. Keep all valuables out of sight. If you are walking at night, wear light-colored clothing. If you do a lot of walking—or jogging—purchase a reflective vest, and wear it even during the day. At night, confine your walks to well-lit, well-traveled areas. Day or night, if you are walking on a road without a sidewalk, always walk *facing* oncoming traffic. Avoid wearing earphones; they reduce your awareness both physically and psychologically. Always try to walk with a friend, especially at night.

Have an escape plan in mind. If you think you are being followed, observed, or stalked, head for the nearest safe place—a public area or building, such as a store. If you still don't feel safe, call 911.

At the ATM

After he was caught, the celebrated Depression-era safe cracker and bank robber Willie Sutton was supposedly asked by a reporter, "Why do you rob banks?" His answer (it's said) was simple: "Because that's where they keep the money."

Today, Willie's answer would be obsolete. These days, "they" keep the money on almost every other street corner or storefront. Hundreds of thousands of ATMs dispense cash practically everywhere and any time, 24 hours a day, 7 days a week. A thief need only watch and wait for someone to approach an ATM—and then make his move.

ATM Robbery: Just the Facts

At walk-up ATMs, most holdups happen at night, between 7 P.M. and midnight. The typical ATM robber is a male under 25 years old. He usually works alone. Typically, the robber will position himself near a machine—within 50 feet—and wait for a victim to approach and withdraw cash. About half of the robberies are carried out after the withdrawal, as the victim steps away from the machine. Most thieves are savvy enough to know that ATMs are camera equipped. They don't want to be recorded. Nevertheless, about half the robbers force the victim to withdraw a large amount of money.

Bad Idea!

If an assailant claims to have a concealed weapon, don't assume he's bluffing. Take him at his word. If he wants money, give him money.

Most victims are women, alone. Almost all victims report that they never saw the robber coming. Stealth is a big part of this crime. Typically, an ATM holdup is armed robbery—or, at least, the thief will claim to have a gun or other concealed weapon.

Countermeasures

Before ATMs began to proliferate in the mid-1970s, people had to plan their cash needs in advance, making a trip to the bank—during regular banking hours—to withdraw what they required. Today, we can get the cash we want whenever and wherever we want it. Robbers know that, too.

Make a return to the "good old days" of your parents and grandparents. Plan your cash needs in advance, so that you will not have to use ATMs in questionable locations and at odd hours—especially at night.

When you must use a machine at night, choose one that is in a brightly lit, high-traffic location. A very good choice is a machine inside a busy supermarket. The next best is a drive-up ATM, which are inherently safer than walk-up machines. Shift the car into park while you transact your business, but do keep the motor running. Avoid ATMs that seem to be positioned in remote locations, such as behind buildings, pillars, or walls, generally screened from full public view.

Remember, most victims report having been completely unaware of the robber's presence. Whether in your car or on foot, look around before you approach the ATM. Identify any hiding spots, and take note of lurkers. ATM robbers often like to stake out machines located near freeway on-ramps or other high-speed thoroughfares, so that they can make a fast getaway.

 Safe Move

Somebody just hanging out near the ATM you want to use? Move on to another machine.

It goes without saying that you should memorize your PIN (personal identification number). Never carry that number with you. Approach the machine with your ATM card ready. After you insert your card and key in your PIN, look behind and around you. A robber will approach from behind or from the side.

Never accept a request for help from a stranger at the ATM—especially if the person making the request is a male. Just say "I'm sorry" and move on.

Stay Alert

If you see someone suspicious approaching while you are at the ATM terminal, cancel your transaction and leave—fast. Trust your gut.

If the potential assailant closes in on you, start running—even if it means leaving your card in the machine. Before you take off, loudly tell the person to back off and leave you alone. A robber does not expect this. It may startle him sufficiently to buy you an extra second or two to run.

The Transaction and After

Whenever you key in your PIN, take care to hide your keystrokes from prying eyes. When you key in your number, hunch over and even use your free hand to screen your keyboard hand. "Shoulder surfing" is the art of peering over someone's shoulder and taking note of what ATM keys are being pressed. Shoulder surfers work in teams, one thief shoulder surfing the victim's PIN, and another picking his pocket to get at his ATM card soon after the victim steps away from the machine. This may be a nonviolent form of ATM robbery—but it still hurts.

After you receive your cash, put it away immediately. Do not pause to count it. You can do this later—besides, these machines are almost never wrong. Make sure you extract your card and receipt. Then walk briskly away.

If You Are Confronted

No amount of cash is worth your life or injury. If a robber demands your money, give it to him. If he demands that you use your card to take money out of the ATM, do so. Then get to a safe place and call the police immediately. Do not follow or chase the robber.

The Case for Public Transportation

Depending where you grew up and what you're used to, taking public transportation—buses, rapid transit trains, subways—may make you *feel* less safe than driving from place to place in your own car. The fact is, however, that public transportation is not only cheaper than automobile travel, it is also ecologically more responsible, and it is almost certainly safer than automobile travel. Nevertheless, there is some risk from crowds and from the absence of crowds.

In a crowded train, bus, or depot, you run a slight risk of injury and a somewhat more significant risk of getting your pocket picked or your purse snatched. When you take a bus or ride a train late at night, you can feel isolated and vulnerable—and, in fact, you may be.

Ever Vigilant

Some of us love riding on buses and subways. We find it fun and fascinating to "people watch." Some of us, however, tend to get lost in our own thoughts while riding. On purpose or unconsciously, we tune out our surroundings. Still others among us tend to drowse and nod off. Neither of these last two responses are safe strategies for riding the public transit system.

Remember, bad actors go bad for any number of reasons. They develop a variety of techniques for committing their crimes, but they all have one thing in common. They choose victims who look preoccupied, out of it, unaware.

Don't look that way. Don't be that way.

Danger Points

Statistically, the most hazardous part of travel on public transportation takes place before or after you board a bus or a train. The mad dash to catch that bus may lead you to jaywalk, to ignore traffic dangers, to trip, to fall, or to make someone else fall. In subway stations, steep stairs and escalators can be hazardous, especially in crowds and especially if you are loaded down with packages. Watch where you are going. Keep at least one hand free for the handrail.

Staying Safe En Route

Try to schedule your public transit travel during normal business hours. Avoid late night and the wee hours of the morning. If possible, choose the most popular bus stops. In subway stations, use the main entrances and exits. Avoid byways, long, lonely tunnels, side exits, and other shortcuts.

The most common crimes on mass transit are pickpocketing and purse snatching—which also includes the taking of briefcases, laptops, hand luggage, and even musical instrument cases. Keep a tight grip on purses and other items. If the item has a shoulder strap, put it on your shoulder so that the strap crosses your chest; in other words, if the strap goes over your left shoulder, the bag should hang on your right side. Never carry your wallet in your back (hip) pocket. Keep it either in your side pocket or in an inside jacket pocket.

If you can grab a window seat, do so. Then put your purse, briefcase, or other hand luggage between you and the window. If you are on the aisle, put your stuff on your lap, with your arms on top of it.

If you must stand, use one hand to hold the bar or strap and the other to carry your purse or briefcase.

Don't wear flashy jewelry or gold neck chains. Take them off and hide them while in transit. You can always put them back on later—if you really want to wear them.

Keep your eyes moving. Watch what's going on. Let others see that you are alert.

Safe Move

If a stranger asks you a question, by all means be polite—but also be brief and businesslike. An overly friendly approach from a stranger may signal that you are in the presence of one-half of a pickpocketing or purse-snatching team—the half whose job it is to engage and distract you. On the other hand, you are in a confined space for a certain period, and you do not want to provoke a confrontation by ignoring a question or being rude.

The Kindness of Strangers

Surely you think you're old enough to have outgrown your parents' warning not to talk to strangers. However, don't turn your back on that advice entirely. If a stranger asks you a question or engages you in conversation, you don't have to clam up or run away, but you should keep your distance. You want to give yourself ample time to react—to move—if the stranger suddenly shows hostile intentions.

Be wary of any advice a stranger gives you, especially if you haven't asked for it. Street crooks typically work in teams, with one felon doing the set up, and the other—or others—doing the crime. A stranger who advises you that you can buy a $10 Rolex from a guy down that alley is very likely setting you up for something you do not want.

The Least You Need to Know

◆ Crimes and accidents that happen outside of the campus occur on campus as well. Your best defense, on or off campus, is awareness and vigilance.

◆ Driving on a college campus requires extra caution because of the large number of pedestrians present and the likelihood that many other drivers will be distracted or preoccupied.

◆ Getting into or out of your parked car may put you at risk in certain situations. Be vigilant. Get in and out without delay.

◆ Use common sense and positive body language when you walk, especially if you are walking alone in off hours.

◆ Plan your cash needs so that you do not have to use ATMs at night or in questionable locations.

◆ When using public transit, take care to avoid accidents on stairways and escalators and keep a close watch on wallets, purses, laptop computers, and the like.

Chapter 8

Drink and Drugs

In This Chapter

- ◆ Alcohol, drugs, and the law
- ◆ Alcohol, drugs, and your health
- ◆ Alcohol, drugs, and personal responsibility
- ◆ The dangers of binge drinking
- ◆ DUI
- ◆ Help with alcohol and drug problems

It's hard to argue that all the laws concerning alcohol, marijuana, and controlled substances make perfect sense and are uniformly effective, but they exist for a reason. Consumption of these substances entails such risk that lawmakers and the citizens who elect them believe that they must be strictly regulated. If using the substances themselves can profoundly affect your life, your health, and your future, so can violating the laws regulating them.

What the Law Says

Attitudes toward drink and drugs vary, but the law is the law. The wisdom of the law can be debated, but we will not do that here. The law concerning alcohol and drugs is the law, and so we begin with the facts.

Alcohol

In 1919, three fourths of states that make up the United States ratified the Eighteenth Amendment to the Constitution, making it illegal to manufacture, sell, buy, or consume alcoholic beverages anywhere in the nation. The result of Prohibition was that, overnight, America became a country of lawbreakers, as people continued to manufacture, sell, and consume beer, wine, and hard liquor, bringing to birth in the process a massive system of organized crime to supply the nation's illicit needs. In 1933, ratification of the Twenty-first Amendment repealed the Eighteenth, and Prohibition came to an end. For a time, the federal government essentially withdrew from the regulation of alcohol, leaving it to the states, counties, cities, even wards and precincts within cities to establish laws concerning drink. All of these local jurisdictions took into account local customs and values and passed laws and ordinances accordingly.

In recent years, the federal government got involved again, in effect making 21 the national legal minimum drinking age by tying federal highway funds to state laws mandating that minimum age. Any state is free to set a lower minimum drinking age, but it will forfeit its federal highway money if it does. Predictably, not a single state has voted to lower the drinking age.

The laws apply to the vendors of alcohol as well as to those who consume it. State and local laws regulating the consumption of alcohol in private—in one's own home or in someone else's home—vary, but in public (including bars and clubs), if you are under 21 and have alcohol in your body, you are illegally in possession of alcohol. If you are holding a drink, you are illegally in possession of alcohol. If you are holding an open beer bottle outdoors, you are not only illegally in possession of alcohol, you are most likely in violation of the "open container" laws.

Most jurisdictions prohibit drinking in the street, that is, outside of restaurants, bars, or private property. If you are illegally in possession of alcohol—even if you are not intoxicated—you are subject to arrest and prosecution.

Marijuana and Controlled Substances

Marijuana is illegal, as are controlled substances. This single sentence tells you pretty much all you need to know about drug laws everywhere in the United States, but we can go into some more detail.

Marijuana is the most commonly used controlled substance. Possession of less than 1 ounce of marijuana is usually considered a misdemeanor or an ordinance violation. Possession of more than an ounce typically takes the violator into felony territory. What is the difference? Felonies are crimes punishable by more than one year in jail. Misdemeanors are crimes punishable by less than one year in jail. Ordinance violations are also punishable by less than one year in jail but, in practice, usually involve very little or no jail time;

> **Little Black Book**
>
> A "controlled substance" is a drug or chemical whose possession and use are regulated under the Controlled Substances Act, enacted into law by Congress as Title II of the Comprehensive Drug Abuse Prevention and Control Act of 1970. Go to www.usdoj.gov/dea/pubs/csa.html for the full text of this act, including a list of the substances to which it applies.

those convicted are typically sentenced to serve some number of hours of community service. This means you can wear your college colors while picking up trash on the side of the road.

Why do various jurisdictions distinguish between felony and lesser penalties in regard to marijuana? The substance is so commonly used that many local jurisdictions enact policies that make it easier to prosecute a violator for some crime by giving up on the idea of putting that violator away for a long time. Lest this make you more willing to risk arrest for marijuana possession, think hard. Although the penalties for violating the marijuana laws are in many places less severe than they once were, the case of obtaining a conviction is proportionately much greater. In other words, if you are caught, you probably will be convicted, but you will not be given a long jail sentence.

Bad Idea!

If you are arrested or issued a summons for possession of marijuana, don't appear in court without an attorney who is familiar with your case and who has advised you on how to plead.

These days, people in possession of a small amount of marijuana may not even be arrested, but only issued a summons—a ticket—ordering a court appearance. Some defendants choose to plead guilty because the penalties for simple possession are usually comparatively trivial, whereas the risk of prosecutorial and judicial vengeance is high for those who take a case to trial and lose.

Possession of controlled substances, such as cocaine, methamphetamine, heroin, and other drugs listed on the controlled substances list that is part of the Controlled Substances Act, carry more severe penalties than marijuana possession. Don't make the mistake of thinking you are living in Amsterdam, where marijuana is legal and many other drugs largely decriminalized. Although the attitudes of police and prosecutors may vary from place to place, the penalties everywhere in this country are severe for possession of controlled substances.

These days, we've become accustomed to news stories about celebrities who are arrested for drug violations only to "get off" with a stint in a rehab center that resembles a luxury spa far more than it does a hospital. Don't make the mistake of believing that you will be treated like a celebrity. Even if you escape jail time, a conviction for any drug offense will dog you for the rest of your life. Whatever judicial penalty you receive, you may also suffer loss of scholarship money, loss of athletic eligibility, academic suspension, or even expulsion. A record of drug conviction does not help you get a job after college, either.

Your Health

Let's say you're about 18 years old. That means you think you are going to live, in perfect health, forever. Intellectually, you know that's not true, but, because you're 18, it's what you nevertheless believe. You can't help it.

One thing you probably don't know is that your habits now will become your lifestyle later. Consuming alcohol and using controlled substances can adversely impact your health.

What Happens When You Drink

When you take a drink, the alcohol is immediately absorbed into your bloodstream. Unlike most other substances you ingest, alcohol does not require digestion before it is absorbed and circulated. While it circulates throughout the body, alcohol is diffused in proportion to the water content of the various tissues and organs, appearing in greatest concentration in the blood and the brain.

Your body gets to work quickly trying to eliminate the alcohol that has been taken in. A small amount is exhaled with your breath, and a somewhat larger amount is secreted in sweat. Quite a bit more is excreted by the kidneys, which is why the restroom doorway is always the most crowded spot at the local club.

But it's a losing battle. No more than 10 percent of the alcohol you ingest is eliminated through breathing, sweating, and urination. The rest—that is, 90 percent or more—is metabolized, mostly by the liver. In this organ, enzymes convert the alcohol to acetate, which enters the bloodstream and is eventually transformed into carbon dioxide and water and then disposed of.

In a 21-year-old man of average height and weight, about half an ounce of alcohol—which is the equivalent of an ounce of hard liquor, a 12-ounce bottle of beer, or a 4-ounce glass of wine—is metabolized per hour. This means that if you drink more than one drink per hour, unmetabolized alcohol accumulates in the bloodstream, affecting your organs—especially your brain. You get drunk. Maybe you get sick.

Say you drink 4 ounces of 100-proof vodka in an hour, thereby consuming 1.5 ounces of alcohol. By the end of the hour, you have a blood alcohol concentration (BAC) of 0.07 percent. Drink another 4 ounces in the next hour, and your BAC goes up to 0.11 percent.

You are officially loaded—and significantly impaired. At 0.05 BAC, inhibitions fade and judgment becomes clouded. At 0.10, speech is slurred, staggering is apparent. You are drunk.

The following standard table shows you what you can expect at various blood alcohol levels:

Immediate Effects of Alcohol Consumption

BAC (percent)	Probable Effect
.05	Loss of inhibitions; clouded judgment
.10	Impairment of coordination; staggering; slurred speech; visual impairment
.20	Senses dulled; loss of control over emotions
.30	"Blackout" (memory impairment); possible loss of consciousness
.35–.45	Coma; possible death
.60	Probable death

The following standard table shows you how much drinking it takes to get to each BAC level:

Alcohol Consumption, Gender, Weight, and BAC

Alcohol	Drinks/ hour*	Female 100 lbs.	Female 150 lbs.	Male 150 lbs.	Male 200 lbs.
½ oz.	1	.045	.03	.025	.019
1 oz.	2	.09	.06	.05	.037
2 oz.	4	.18	.12	.10	.07
3 oz.	6	.27	.18	.15	.11
4 oz.	8	.36	.24	.20	.15
5 oz.	10	.45	.30	.25	.18

Drink = 1 oz. 100-proof spirits, 12 oz. beer, or 5 oz. wine

How Drinking Affects Your Health

In the short run, overindulgence in alcohol creates a hangover (headache, nausea, vomiting, and possibly other symptoms) as well as temporarily impaired judgment, temporarily impaired reflexes, and temporarily impaired coordination. If you are drunk, you will likely make some stupid, destructive, and possibly lethal decisions. If you get behind the wheel while under the influence of alcohol (or controlled substances), you may injure or kill yourself and/or others.

In the longer term, drinking in moderation has never been shown to cause disease in normal, healthy people; however, frequent drinking to the point of moderate intoxication—a noticeable "buzz"—can eventually damage the tissues of the mouth, esophagus, and stomach, and may increase your chances of developing cancer. Because the liver is the primary target of alcohol, this organ may be seriously damaged by repeated bouts of drunkenness. Heart muscle may also suffer.

Drinking to excess over a prolonged period creates nutritional problems, including weight gain without deriving the nutritional value supplied by food. And, finally, people who drink a lot tend to look worn out, haggard, and just plain old.

Bad Idea!

If you are pregnant or think you are pregnant, it is critically important that you avoid all alcoholic beverages. Drinking alcohol in any amount is dangerous to the development of the fetus.

Alcoholism

You are never too young to be an alcoholic. Over the years, experts have debated the definition of alcoholism, but most agree on this much: alcoholism is the repetitive intake of alcoholic beverages to such an extent that repeated or continued harm to the drinker occurs.

Most medical authorities classify alcoholism as a disease, and there is evidence that the condition is at least in part hereditary.

Are you an alcoholic? According to Alcoholics Anonymous, if you exhibit any of the following signs, consult a physician:

1. You indulge in binges—bouts of uncontrolled or clearly excessive drinking.

2. You drink for the purpose of getting drunk.

3. You are unable to stop drinking after one or two drinks.

4. You need to consume greater and greater quantities of alcohol to achieve the same effect.

5. You suffer problems caused by drinking: inability to concentrate on your job; lateness and absenteeism; arguments with colleagues, friends, and family.

6. You avoid family and friends when drinking.

7. You become irritated when your drinking is discussed by family and friends.

8. You are unable to keep promises made to yourself about curbing your drinking.

9. You feel guilty or remorseful about your drinking.

10. You "black out" frequently—can't remember what you did while you were drinking.

11. You eat irregularly during periods of drinking.

12. You use drinking to escape your problems.

What happens to alcoholics?

In the short run, they may suffer everything from really bad hangovers to delirium tremens, the so-called "DTs." DT symptoms resemble heroin withdrawal and include convulsive shaking, fever, uncontrollable panic, and terrifying hallucinations.

Hard Fact

A number of medical studies in recent years have suggested that there are some positive health benefits derived from moderate alcohol consumption, including reduced risk of heart attack. Some studies suggest that moderate consumers of alcohol have a 10 percent lower death rate from all causes than do total abstainers. We invite you to investigate all these and all other claims concerning your health. One thing is for certain, however. All scientific studies that claim any health benefits from moderate alcohol consumption apply only to adults, 21 and over.

In the longer term, alcoholics may develop a degenerative disease of the nervous system known as polyneuropathy, or other irreversible diseases of the central nervous system. Liver diseases, including acute hepatitis (inflammation of the liver) and cirrhosis (scarring of the liver tissue), are common.

Alcoholics suffer high accident rates and are more susceptible to infection than nonalcoholics.

Marijuana and Your Health

We're pretty sure that neither your parents nor your grandparents want you to smoke marijuana, but it's also likely that they come from a time and a culture that was more accepting of marijuana than most of society is at present. At the very least, they may believe that, whatever else may be good or bad about pot, a little reefer won't harm your physical health.

The fact is that smoking marijuana is more damaging to your health than smoking tobacco, which, as we know, causes cancer and heart disease. Other effects on your health include, in the short term, problems with memory and learning; distorted perception; difficulty in thinking and problem solving; loss of coordination; and increased heart rate. In the longer term, recent research suggests that marijuana abuse creates changes in the brain similar to those seen after long-term abuse of other major drugs.

At least one recent study (by the National Institute on Drug Abuse, an agency of the National Institutes of Health) has indicated that frequent marijuana use quadruples the risk of heart attack in the first hour after smoking marijuana. A recent study of 450 individuals concluded that people who smoke marijuana frequently but do not smoke tobacco have more health problems and miss more days of work than nonsmokers. Even occasional use can cause burning and stinging of the mouth and throat, often accompanied by a severe cough. Regular marijuana use typically causes the same respiratory problems that are common among tobacco smokers, and it's possible that smoking marijuana increases the likelihood of developing cancer of the head or neck. As with cigarette smoking, the use of marijuana has the potential to promote cancer of the lungs and other parts of the respiratory tract. Marijuana smoke contains 50 to 70 percent more carcinogenic hydrocarbons than does tobacco smoke.

Regular or frequent marijuana use is especially bad for college students because, in addition to intensifying such existing problems as depression and anxiety, marijuana significantly compromises the ability to learn and remember information. The more you use marijuana, the more likely you are to fall behind in building intellectual, job, or social skills. Most disturbing is research indicating that the adverse impact of marijuana on memory and learning may last for days or even weeks after the acute effects of the drug wear off.

Hard Fact

A recent study of 129 college students found that, among those who smoked marijuana at least 27 of the 30 days prior to being surveyed, skills related to attention, memory, and learning were significantly impaired, even after the students had not taken the drug for at least 24 hours. If you smoke marijuana every day, you are probably functioning at a reduced intellectual level all of the time.

Defenders of marijuana have long pointed out that, unlike many other drugs, pot is not addictive. This has been contradicted by much recent research, which shows that long-term marijuana abuse can lead to addiction for some people—provided that "addiction" is defined as the compulsive use of the drug even though it interferes with family, school, work, and recreational activities. Marijuana is also a "gateway drug." To be sure, not all frequent marijuana users go on to use other, "harder" drugs, but many drug users also use—or have used—marijuana.

Other Controlled Substances

The dangers from narcotics and controlled substances other than marijuana are so dire and dramatic that we cannot even begin to list them in detail. They range from addiction and addiction-related symptoms to death.

Quite possibly the greatest risk to your health comes from the people you have to associate with to obtain illegal substances. Count on it: your local pusher is not a member of the Better Business Bureau. Cross him, and he will kill you. If you don't pay, you *will* pay.

Life offers precious few mulligans. You don't get the opportunity to start fresh after every mistake.

Your Career—Now and Later

Maybe you've already had some experience with alcohol and drugs in high school. One or both may even have been significant and quite possibly regarded—by you or others—as a problem. Even if this was the case, things were different back then.

You were younger.

Society is generous with the room it gives for error—as long as you're a kid. Most of the decisions you make and the actions you take prior to age 17 will not follow you into your later years. Once your seventeenth year ends, however, the picture changes dramatically. Put it this way: just about anything you do after 17 will follow you for as long as you live.

There is a current theme among sociologists and popular pundits that goes something like this: "30 is the new 21." The thought is that, these days, young people mature later, and it takes until 30 to actually become an adult. Maybe this works as the current explanation and excuse for immature behavior, but it won't wash in court. From 18 on, count on "the system" treating you as an adult. You will be held fully accountable for your criminal conduct.

Many colleges and universities are beginning to accept responsibility for having created campus environments that manage the use of alcohol and controlled substances poorly. They have little choice. The courts have begun holding school officials criminally complicit in cases involving the illegal use of alcohol and drugs. With the pressure ratcheted up on school administrators, you can be sure that they will, in turn, be harder on you than they were on the students just a class or two ahead of you.

The days of turning a blind eye on bad behavior are coming to an end. This means that more and more emphasis will be placed on internal judicial processes, with or without the involvement of the police. That is not necessarily a break for you. Make an admission of guilt to an administrator or admit responsibility regarding behavior that could be construed as criminal, and you may find your confession or admission used against you in court. Just because your school may try to handle a misdeed internally does not mean you're safe from the criminal justice system.

However bad behavior is handled in the short term—by school administration or by the cops and the courts—you are still liable to pay the price and to keep on paying for a very long time. No school, graduate school, or employer is eager to make space for a man or a woman with a criminal record.

The "Social" Drinker and the "Binge" Drinker

Okay. Buying and using illegal drugs and controlled substances is bad. And you don't do it or ever intend to do it. But drinking? *Everybody* drinks, including your parents. They aren't drunks. They aren't alcoholics. They aren't ruining their lives. They're just "social drinkers."

There was a time when social drinking was popular on college campuses. Young folks got together, some too young to drink, of course, but they did it anyway. It was illegal, but there was probably no great harm in it, because the purpose of these occasions was to talk and to socialize—people just enjoying each other's company in a relaxed setting made even more relaxed by a little beer.

Those days are gone. These days, college drinkers, male and female alike, "pound" their beers with the abandon of a sailor on short-term liberty. It's called binge drinking, and it's the mode of choice for alcohol consumption on most campuses.

Binge drinking is incredibly dangerous and equally appealing. Your friends will encourage you to participate in it, and you will be tempted to do so. Moreover—and paradoxically—the zero-tolerance approach that society has taken toward underage alcohol consumption actually encourages you to drink as much as you can as fast as you can, before someone turns off the tap. On many campuses, the goal is to get drunk in the shortest amount of time possible and to hope for the best.

The "best" is a lot to hope for. You should consider that, once upon a time, it was usually possible to drink, act stupid, fall asleep somewhere safe, and forget about it the next day—at least after your wicked hangover began to fade. Today, however, it's more likely that you will get sick, fall down, pass out in some compromising position or state of undress, and the next day you (along with the rest of the world) can view photos of yourself in varying stages of inebriation on Facebook. Such images will certainly embarrass you in the short run, and they may follow you for a very long time to come.

Embarrassment, now and in times to come, may be the least of the consequences of binge drinking. Review "What Happens When You Drink" earlier in this chapter to get a picture of the immediate physiological consequences of consuming more than a half-ounce of alcohol—the equivalent of 12 ounces of beer—in an hour.

Lucky for you, your body does not want to die. You'll probably pass out before you have downed enough beer, wine, or hard liquor to kill yourself. Probably. But it's more than theoretically possible to do yourself in by acute alcohol poisoning. It happens to people every year, every semester.

But let's say you survive. The old joke about going to the bar to kill a few brain cells is not really all that funny. Recent research has shown that binge drinking can seriously and permanently damage your brain, especially since—at age 18 or so—your brain is still physically developing. Sustained learning difficulty and memory loss may last your whole life.

DUI/DOA

The statistics speak loudly. Nearly 20,000 people are killed each year in the United States in alcohol-related automobile accidents. Of this number, approximately 7,000 are nondrinking victims. The cost of alcohol-related accidents, in terms of legal, medical, and property expenses, is about $16 billion per year.

Most states have established standards for defining intoxication based on blood alcohol concentration (BAC). In many states, you are deemed intoxicated—and therefore illegally driving under the influence (DUI)—if your BAC is .10 percent or higher; in some states, the level is .08 percent. But get this: all 50 states have BAC limits under .02 percent for drivers under age 21. In Alaska, Arizona, District of Columbia, Illinois, Minnesota, North Carolina, Oregon, Utah, and Wisconsin, even a BAC of .00 may result in a DUI charge against drivers under age 21 if officers find any evidence of alcohol consumption.

Legal penalties for DUI range from fines, license suspensions, and license revocations to serious jail time, but as bad as getting caught is, the legal consequences of DUI are far less terrible than the potential human consequences: loss of life, injury, permanent disability, shattered families, and devastated finances.

Hard Fact
According to 2006 data from the National Highway Traffic Safety Administration (NHTSA), there is a 41 percent chance that *you* will be involved in an alcohol-related car wreck at some point in your life.

According to the NHTSA, at just .05 percent BAC, you are two to three times more likely to become involved in an automobile accident than you are at .00 percent BAC. At .08 percent, you are five to six times more likely to get into a wreck. At .10 percent, your risk jumps to seven to eight times the risk at .00 percent. Beyond this, if your BAC is higher than .10 percent, you are 20 to 50 times more likely to get into an accident.

Getting Help

If you think you have a problem with alcohol or drugs—or if others have told you you have a problem—you can get help. On campus, visit your student health center or counseling service (see Chapter 14), or visit the office of the Dean of Students. By law, everything you tell a medical professional is strictly confidential, even if he or she works for your university. Your campus may also have dedicated alcohol and drug counseling programs available. Check out the college or university website.

Little Black Book
The student health and counseling facilities on your campus are your best and nearest resources for help with alcohol and drug issues. You can also consult the online Substance Abuse Treatment Facility Locator maintained by the U.S. Department of Health and Human Services at http://dasis3.samhsa.gov.

Help is available, but like everything else involving your safety and security, the responsibility for seeking that help is yours. Ask.

The Least You Need to Know

♦ The enforcement of laws governing alcohol and drugs varies, but essentially, possession of alcohol by anyone under 21 is illegal and possession of marijuana and controlled substances by anyone of any age is also illegal.

♦ Abuse of alcohol, marijuana, and other drugs adversely affects health in the short term as well as the long term. Much of the impact is on the brain, including impairment of memory and the ability to learn.

♦ From the age of 18 on, society—including schools and the courts—is very unforgiving when it comes to violations of the law, including the law as it relates to alcohol and drugs.

♦ Binge drinking—drinking heavily in a short period of time—is very dangerous and quite possibly lethal.

♦ Even drinking a small amount of alcohol significantly multiplies your chances of having an accident while driving. The laws of all 50 states have harsh penalties for underage drinkers who drive under the influence.

♦ Help with alcohol and drug problems is widely available, including on your campus. But you must take the first step—by *asking* for it.

Chapter 9

Spring Break

In This Chapter

◆ Spring break traditions and destinations

◆ The long—and local—arm of the law

◆ How to have a "street smart" spring break

◆ Avoiding spring break travel-package scams

◆ Tips for international travel

◆ Creative alternatives to the traditional spring break

Sun, surf, parties, booze, and sex. For many, this is the list that answers the question, *What is spring break, anyway?* Some of this image is the stuff of myth and legend. Some of it is as true as any blanket generalization can be true (which means that there are exceptions). And some of it, of late, is just plain outdated. As we'll see at the end of this chapter, for a growing number of students, spring break is a time to give back to the community, to lend a helping hand where one is needed, and to feel something more positive than a hangover when the week's up.

What kind of guests motivate a city to pass laws turning them away? Well, certainly not a set of guests that make themselves welcome.

What's It All About?

Fort Lauderdale was the mother of all spring break venues, starting out as the destination of choice for the Colgate University men's swimming team back in 1935. Fort Lauderdale and other sunny venues got a big boost in popularity after the 1960 film comedy *Where the Boys Are* made a big hit with its tale of Midwestern coeds spending spring break in Lauderdale in their (mostly quite successful) effort to meet lots and lots of boys.

In 1985, however, Fort Lauderdale residents decided to put a lid on most of the partying by passing ordinances severely restricting celebratory excesses. The spring breakers got the message and, by 1989, their numbers fell from 350,000 annually to about 20,000. Apparently, that was just fine with the people of Fort Lauderdale, who passed even more stringent regulations in 2006.

After 1985, Daytona Beach, Florida, became the new spring break hot spot, with annual visitation of about 200,000. But even hang-loose Daytona—today still a mecca for bikers—finally had enough of the college crowd, passed some laws, and reduced spring break attendance by the early twenty-first century to a point so low that no one even bothers to make estimates anymore.

Nevertheless, spring break—which may occur as early as the end of February or as late as the end of April—continues strong in many other places and is still about getting some sun on the beach, but drugs—always illegal—and drinking—sometimes underage, sometimes excessive, often both—are usually part of the experience as well. And so, for some party goers, are reckless sex and general bad behavior, including public nudity, vandalism, disorderly conduct, driving under the influence, violence, robbery, rape, and sometimes abduction, disappearance, and murder.

Does a really good time have to be obnoxious, unlawful, and dangerous?

Vacation Venues

In 2007, the most popular spring break spots included Cancun, Rosarito, Puerto Vallarta, and Acapulco, Mexico; South Beach (Miami Beach) and Panama City Beach, Florida; South Padre Island, Texas; Negril, Jamaica;

and Nassau, Bahamas. Most spring breakers fly to these destinations, but an increasingly popular mode of travel is the automobile road trip, from the college cities and towns of the Northeast down to venues in Florida. Making a strong showing of late as well is Las Vegas, Nevada.

The appeal of venues south of the border includes a lower legal drinking age—18 instead of 21—whereas the rising spring break star Las Vegas, despite its reputation as "Sin City," strictly enforces its minimum drinking and gambling age, both 21. The casinos are well aware that failure to enforce the age limits can easily result in the loss of a liquor or gaming license. Without beaches—and without booze or gambling—some spring breakers may find Vegas a disappointing destination.

Local Laws

You wouldn't dream of opening your own front door, walking down the driveway, waving to your next-door neighbor, then urinating on the sidewalk. But public urination is one of the offenses for which local authorities most frequently arrest spring breakers.

Sometimes we do things out of town and on vacation that we would never do close to home. It's as if we believe the local laws somehow don't apply to us when we're far from home or far from campus.

But they do.

We will talk about the laws abroad in a few moments, but for now, just be aware that if something is illegal in the United States, there is a 99 percent certainty that it is also illegal in Mexico or just about any other foreign country you may visit.

As for U.S. spring break venues, the laws you are familiar with wherever you live or go to school are almost certainly the same laws that apply in Florida or Vegas. It's true that some communities—sometimes— relax enforcement of minor misdemeanors during spring break, but you can't count on it.

> **Bad Idea!**
>
> With so many spring break party goers, surely the police can't arrest everybody. They'll wink at a misdemeanor here or there. Right? Maybe, but it's a bad idea to put the cops to the test.

Most commonly, spring breakers are arrested for underage drinking—the minimum age is 21 in Florida and in Nevada—and for providing alcohol to underage drinkers. Fighting is another common offense, as is the ever-popular public urination.

Technically speaking, there is no federally mandated minimum drinking age in the United States, but the National Minimum Drinking Age Act of 1984 withholds revenue from states that allow the purchase of alcohol to anyone under the age of 21. This has proven sufficient to prompt all 50 states to enact laws prohibiting the underage purchase of alcohol. Some states prohibit those under 21 from even being present in liquor stores or in bars, but a few states prohibit alcohol consumption by minors in private settings—namely in private residences. New York State permits those under 21 to drink in restaurants, as long as they are accompanied by a parent or guardian who actually pours the drink. As of 2007, 20 states do not explicitly ban underage consumption, and even among those that do, 15 make certain exceptions.

Law on the Beach

As for the beach, special ordinances typically apply. In Florida, for example, no alcoholic beverages of any kind are allowed on public beaches—no matter how old you are. No glass containers are permitted (glass breaks and broken glass causes injuries). No overnight sleeping or camping is permitted on beaches. Except in specially designated areas, no fires are allowed. Many beach communities also prohibit overnight sleeping in automobiles.

Safe Move

We all need—and most of us crave—a certain amount of sun. Too much, however, can cause dangerous burns, sunstroke (potentially fatal), and—cumulatively—skin cancer. Limit sun exposure during peak sun hours, 10 A.M. to 4 P.M. Seek shade. Trees and umbrellas block about 60 percent of the sun's rays. A wide-brimmed hat, sunglasses, and long-sleeved, tightly woven clothing also offer good protection. Exposed skin should be slathered liberally with broad-spectrum sunscreens whose active ingredients block both UVA and UVB rays. Use products that offer a minimum Sun Protective Factor (SPF) of 15.

Sin City?

Partly as a result of its own efforts at self-promotion, Las Vegas is universally perceived as a Sin City, which many take to believe includes an absence of law or, at least, of law enforcement.

Not true.

Perhaps the most commonly held myth about Las Vegas is that prostitution is legal. While it's true that Nevada has no state law prohibiting prostitution, plenty of Nevada communities, including Clark County, home of Las Vegas, strictly outlaw it. Not only is prostitution illegal in Las Vegas, the law is very strictly enforced.

Liquor, it is also said, flows freely in Vegas. Well, there is a lot of it, but you have to be 21 to drink—and bars, restaurants, and casinos are very rigorous in enforcement. At the very least, underage drinking will bring down a heavy fine; far worse, every bar, restaurant, and casino employee is acutely aware that his or her job is on the line if an underage drinker gets by on his or her watch. Management is even more acutely aware that the gaming and liquor licenses of the establishment hang by a thread.

Just as you must be at least 21 to drink in a Vegas casino, you must be at least that old to gamble. This law is enforced vigilantly, especially during spring break.

Vegas Pot

Another Vegas myth is that, in Nevada, a licensed physician can legally prescribe "medical marijuana." Actually, that myth had a basis in truth—at least until the U.S. Supreme Court struck down the Nevada law permitting the medical use of marijuana. Since the high court's decision, no one, regardless of credentials, can legally prescribe pot. In fact, despite being the home state of Sin City, Nevada is a mostly very conservative place, a very "red" state, with drug laws that are some of the harshest in the United States. And they are very stringently enforced in Las Vegas, especially during spring break.

A Street-Smart Spring Break

Just as the 2007 shootings at Virginia Tech made campus safety a topic of urgent concern, so the disappearance of Natalee Holloway on May 30, 2005, during a high school graduation trip to the island of Aruba has made many think carefully about personal safety on college vacations, especially spring break. The most productive response to tragedies such as those at Virginia Tech and in Aruba is not fear and avoidance, but preparation, common sense, and—even on vacation—vigilance.

Prepare to Have Fun

A spur-of-the-moment vacation is a seductive notion, but it's usually not a good idea, especially on spring break. Make a plan. Decide where you are going, then do a little research before you set off. Scope out the good and the bad about your destination. Is crime a particular problem? Vacation-time overcrowding?

If you're going to a foreign country, do you speak the language? And how widely spoken is English? What are the drug laws? How are they enforced? Some vacation destinations have very strict laws concerning both drugs and the abuse of alcohol, and officials may specifically target young offenders. Some foreign law enforcement agencies are notoriously corrupt and are not above such practices as entrapment and solicitation of bribes.

Safe Move

When you travel abroad, be sure you know enough of the local language to summon the police or medical aid. At the very least, know how to say "Help me."

Don't leave for spring break without making sure that your family has your full itinerary, including all hotels, flight numbers, and the like, and also has multiple phone numbers for you: your cell phone, travel companions' phones, and so on. For added security, it's a very good idea to photocopy your passport, your driver's license, and your credit cards (front and back), and leave these documents in the care of your family. Keep family members updated concerning any change of plans.

It's hardly news to the average college student that cell phones have come to play a huge part in our lives. They are especially important when traveling, since they provide a big measure of convenience and security. Depending on your phone and your cell phone company plan, your cell may or may not work outside of the United States. If you are planning spring break abroad, set up international service in advance. Don't simply assume that the phone and the plan you have now will work abroad. Don't wait until you're in trouble far from home to discover the limitations of your equipment and service. Many cell phone providers will sell you service to cover just the duration of your trip. Call customer service.

Being There

Spring break is all about togetherness. It is not a time for solitary wandering. They say two's company and three's a crowd. Not so for spring breakers. It's safest—and probably the most fun—to travel in groups of three or even more. Why is three the minimum? If one of you gets in trouble, one of the two remaining can stay behind while the other goes for help.

A lot of the appeal of travel is the opportunity to meet new people. Just beware of blindly trusting strangers. It is never a good idea to accept an invitation to go off alone with a person you've just met. You would not do this in your hometown or your college community. Why would you do this on vacation?

Guard your personal information. Do not freely share with brand-new acquaintances the particulars of where you are staying. Do not accept rides in unmarked taxis.

Watch what you eat and drink. In some foreign destinations, food and drink may be of questionable sanitary quality. Eat at reputable restaurants, and drink bottled water or bottled soft drinks. If you are of age and are drinking at a bar, get your drinks directly from the bartender and don't leave your drink unattended. The stories you may have heard about "date rape" drugs, whatever the accuracy or inaccuracy of the details, are based on fact. These drugs exist and they come in a great variety, the most common being GHB and Rohypnol. Rohypnol is also known as *circles, the forget-me pill, La Rocha, lunch money drug, R-2, rib, roach-2, rope, robutal, rophies, row-shay, ruffles, wolfies,* and (most frequently) *roofies.*

Date rape drugs induce anesthesia and facilitate rape by significantly incapacitating the victim, rendering her incapable of resisting or even saying no. In effect, roofies paralyze the victim both physically and mentally. Beyond the obvious dangers of rape, the drug's action is made more powerful by combination with alcohol. At the very least, it will probably result in a severe hangover, but may also create what psychologists call anterograde amnesia, in which events that took place when the drug was active are forgotten. Moreover, anytime a depressant-type drug is combined with alcohol, there is danger of a harmful or even fatal overdose.

If you order a drink and it looks or tastes strange, dump it. Drug contamination often (but not invariably) makes the drink taste salty and may visibly cloud the drink or leave a residue floating on top or on the sides of the glass.

Protect yourself from date rape drugs by never taking a beverage from someone you do not know and trust, by never leaving your beverage unattended, and by avoiding the punch bowl. If you believe you have been drugged, get help from the police right away or get to a hospital emergency room. Request a drug screen. The body rapidly metabolizes date rape drugs—usually within 12 hours or less—and therefore may be difficult to detect.

Many spring breakers measure their fun by the level of intoxication they manage to achieve. Getting falling-down drunk is never a very good idea, but it can be downright catastrophic when you're in public. In the jungle, predators look for the weakest and most vulnerable animal in a herd. Human predators operate the very same way. They look for the tipsy and the wasted. Your best defense against them is to appear sober at all times, know where you are, who you are with, and what—exactly—you are doing.

Hard Fact

Binge drinking contributes to the high rate of accidents of various sorts during spring break. During spring break, the average male college student reports consuming 18 alcoholic drinks per day. The average woman consumes 10. Fifty percent of men and 40 percent of women report at least one occasion on which they drank until they became sick or lost consciousness.

Chances are if you are on spring break and you are 21 or older, you are going to drink. Control it. Avoid drinking on an empty stomach. Men should limit themselves to one drink per hour; women, one per 1.5 hours. This will give your body time to metabolize the alcohol and will help keep you from getting falling-down drunk or sick.

Avoid mixing different kinds of drinks. For example, don't chase tequila with beer. If you begin to feel strange—tipsy, sick, dizzy—start slurring your words, or have difficulty walking, stop drinking.

As always, when you are out and about, be alert and trust your instincts. If something about where you are or who you're with doesn't feel right, it probably *isn't* right. Act on your instinct and remove yourself from the situation. If you believe that you're being followed, get yourself to a safe place. Ask for help.

Hotel Safety

Staying in a hotel often gives us a sense of security, but remember that, as with any other place open to the public, hotels present potential hazards.

If possible, scope out the available hotels before you pick yours. Look for such features as electronic guest room locks, the kind you open with a magnetic-strip card. These are much safer than old-fashioned key locks, because the combination automatically changes with each new guest. There is very little chance that someone will have a duplicate key to your room. Moreover, if you lose or misplace your key card, tell someone at the front desk, and the card will be replaced with a new one programmed with a new combination. The lost or stolen card cannot be used to open your door.

Other minimum safety features in any hotel include dead bolt locks and peepholes. Be sure to use them. Hotel doors usually lock automatically when closed, but when you are inside your room, throw the dead bolt as well. If the door is equipped with a chain, use that, too. Admit no one into your room until you have confirmed their identity through the peephole. Look before you open the door. The door to your room must never be opened by anyone unless the guest is absolutely known. Be sure to secure locks on windows and adjoining doors, if any.

Thieves and other predators can be very clever. If someone calls your room and says they are with hotel maintenance and need to come up to repair something, get the caller's name, then call the front desk to verify his or her identity before you admit the person. Confirm with the front desk the legitimacy of the caller's business. Otherwise, do not open the door for anyone you do not know.

A good hotel takes steps to protect your security. If someone calls the switchboard asking for your room number, the operator should simply answer "I'll connect you." He or she should never give the number. If you want to test your hotel's security savvy, call the switchboard from a house phone in the lobby and ask for yourself. Then ask, "What room is she in?" If the operator answers with a room number, you are in a potentially dangerous hotel. The correct answer is always "I'll connect you."

Little Black Book

The website of Detective Kevin Coffey, a noted expert on travel safety and consultant to corporate travelers, offers detailed advice on how to stay safe in hotels. Check it out at www.kevincoffee.com/hotel/hotel_safety.htm.

Another important safety consideration is that every room telephone should allow direct outside dialing. House phones in hallways and lobbies, however, should not permit direct room dialing. Callers should be required to go through the hotel operator and request a room by guest name, not room number.

Look for hotels with well-lit interior hallways, parking structures, and grounds. A hotel parking garage should not have elevators that go directly to guest floors. Parking garage elevators should go to the lobby only.

Finally, check out fire safety. Modern hotels have smoke detectors and sprinklers in all rooms, hallways, and meeting rooms.

Checking In

When you arrive by bus or car at your hotel, be sure to remain with your luggage until it's brought into the lobby. It's easy to become distracted during the check-in process, so keep a close watch on your luggage, purse, and other personal property. Also take care not to leave your wallet or credit card lying on the check-in counter while you complete your registration. Be sure the clerk hands your card back to you.

Registration clerks are trained not to announce your room out loud, but to write it down—usually on the envelope that holds your key card. If the clerk does announce your room number, and you think it has been heard by others, explain your security concern and ask for another room. When you sign the registration card, use only your last name and first initial. Do not furnish information that reveals gender.

Before you leave the check-in desk, tell the clerk not to give out your name and room number: "Please call me if anyone asks about me."

Take a handful of matchbooks or business cards with the name, address, and phone number of your hotel. Carry them with you. If you get lost while you are out and about, you'll always have the address and phone number handy. If you are in a foreign country and don't speak the language, you can always hand the information to a cab driver.

Savvy hotel guests give careful thought to room selection. Ideally, select a room between the fourth and sixth floor. Most fire department ladders cannot reach above the sixth floor. Rooms below the fourth floor, however, may get too much street noise. For security, it is not a best bet to accept a ground-floor room, especially if doors or windows open directly to the outside. In motels, of course, you may have no choice—but, in these cases, try to avoid ground-floor rooms that are directly off the parking lot.

Elevator Safety

In most modern hotels, elevators are equipped with surveillance cameras. Nevertheless, take care. Observe your fellow passengers. If someone doesn't look "right" to you, get out. If someone suspicious boards an elevator, exit as soon as possible. Don't wait for your floor.

Whenever possible, board last and select your floor button last. Stay as close to the elevator control panel as possible. Stay out of the corners. If you are attacked, push as many floor buttons as possible—and get out.

Going Out

When you leave your room, keep the television on. At night, keep a light on with drapes partially open, to suggest that someone is inside. Put the "Do not disturb" sign on the door when you are out.

Store valuables in the hotel's security vault or in an in-room safe, provided that it's equipped with an electronic combination lock rather than a fixed combination or key lock.

Safe Move

If you are a woman returning to your room alone and it's late, ask at the front desk for an escort to accompany you in the elevator and up to your room.

Keep your key card separate from your room number. Memorize your room number, and take the key card out of the envelope on which the number is written. Never display your guest room number in public. A thief can walk by, take note of the number, then ring up fraudulent charges on *your* room number.

When you leave your room, take a minimum of cash. Use credit cards and/or traveler's checks. Tone down your appearance. Avoid flashy jewelry and be careful how you carry expensive-looking cameras. Keep different credit cards in different pockets, and separate these from cash or traveler's checks.

If you have a car, take care in parking lots and parking garages. It's always best to walk to and from the car in groups, especially at night. Never leave valuables in your car. Note also that crooks often target rental cars, figuring that these are most likely to contain valuable items, such as well-stocked luggage.

Fire!

Fire is about the last thing most of us think about when we stay at a hotel, but even in a modern hotel, fire remains a danger. Most American hotels are required by law to post fire exit maps in rooms and hallways. When you first check into your room, orient yourself. Determine where the closest exits are. Check out the location of nearby fire alarms and fire extinguishers as well.

Make sure the smoke detector in your room works. Usually, a small light indicates its operation. If you're in doubt, call the front desk.

Be certain that you can get a direct outside line on your room telephone. If you smell smoke or suspect a fire, call the hotel operator first. Give your name and room number, and explain the problem. If the operator does not answer, call 911 directly.

Even if you only suspect a fire, leave if you can. Don't wait for instructions. If others are sharing your room, get them up and out as well. Agree on a meeting place outside of the hotel.

Hard Fact

Recent figures suggest that about 85 percent of American hotels do not have sprinkler systems, and while precise figures on hotel fires are hard to come by, every year in the United States there are more than 32 million fires, making this mishap the third largest cause of accidental injury and death in the country. One out of every eight accidental deaths is from fire.

Before you open the door, feel it with the back of your hand. Then feel the doorknob. If either the door or the knob is warm, drop to your knees, then open the door very slowly. Be prepared to slam it shut if a cloud of smoke rolls in. If, however, the hallway is clear, head for the exit. Use the stairwell, not the elevator. In a fire, there's a very real possibility that the elevator will stop functioning, trapping passengers. When you leave, take your key, and close the door behind you. This will slow the spread of the fire.

If you are moving through smoke, keep low to the floor, crawling if necessary. Smoke and odorless but lethal carbon monoxide tend to rise. The most breathable air is close to the floor. When you reach the exit, walk quickly down the stairs, holding on to the handrail as you go. If you run into significant smoke in the stairwell, do not try to get through it. Instead, turn around, walk up, and find a smoke-free corridor. Cross to an alternate exit.

If you find that you're unable to leave your room, try to make your presence known. Try the phone first. Call the hotel operator. If there's no answer, call 911—first dialing whatever digit you need to get an outside line. Give the operator or fire department your exact location. Hang a bed sheet from the window as a signal.

While waiting for help, open the window if there's smoke in your room. Fill the bathtub with water, soak every towel and sheet you can find, and stuff them around the door and any vents that let smoke in. If the door and walls are hot, use your ice bucket to bail water on them, keeping them as cool as possible. This will retard the outbreak of fire in your room. If possible, wet down your mattress, put it up against the door, and hold it in place with the dresser. Keep everything wet.

Use a wet towel around your nose and mouth to help filter out smoke.

If you see fire outside of your window, pull down the drapes and move everything flammable away from the window.

Unless you are very close to the ground floor, jumping out of the window may prove fatal. Your best move is to continue fighting the fire and keep on signaling until help arrives.

In Praise of Inhibition

Many college students see spring break as a latter-day Roman orgy— a free pass to cast away all inhibitions. The impulse is strong and inviting, but the fact is that inhibition is a mechanism of survival. In normal circumstances, it keeps us from doing things that may result in arrest, injury, general misery, or even death.

Don't be so eager to let go of inhibition.

Alcohol-related accidents are common and sometimes tragic. If you are drunk, you are much more likely to be the target of crime. If alcohol— or just the freewheeling climate of spring break—leads you to irresponsible sexual activity, you are vulnerable to sexually transmitted diseases or sexual assault.

Travel Scams

Overindulgence, misbehavior, arrest, assault, robbery, burglary, and accidents are not the only potential hazards of spring break. Every year, students fall victim to travel scams—typically package deals that sound just too good to be true (precisely because they *are* too good to be true).

Do your best to deal with a reputable travel agent or packager. Before you deal with XYZ Travel Company, ask others about their experience with the company.

The agency or packager should have a street address—not just a P.O. box and certainly not just an e-mail address. You should absolutely have the name of the airline and flight number in hand before purchasing a spring break package. Additionally, obtain the phone number of the destination hotel, together with a reservation confirmation number; call the hotel and confirm that you have the promised reservations *before* you purchase the travel package.

Little Black Book

It's always a good idea to check up on any business, travel agents and packagers included, with the Better Business Bureau (www.bbb.org). Look for customer complaints, regulatory agency complaints, and other potential problems. Be very careful typing in the name of the agency or packager in question. If you mistype the name, the website may return a clean bill of health on a company with a shady past. The website www.travelsense.org will help you find a reputable travel agent.

Read all fine print before signing a package agreement. You need to know how many people have been booked with you as your hotel roommates. Get this number in writing. Be on the lookout for charges hidden in the finest of the fine print. These include hotel damage deposits, which may represent a significant up-front expense and which you may have difficulty recovering; local hotel taxes, which may not be included in the package price as quoted; parking fees; and other extras.

As always, for any deal you are contemplating, there is a great, universal, invariable, golden rule: if it *sounds* too good to be true, it *is* too good to be true.

International Incidents

In recent years, foreign destinations—most of them in Mexico—have been luring more and more spring breakers. Part of the appeal is the attraction of the exotic, but a number of packagers of Mexican trips most heavily promote the nation's minimum drinking age, just 18, and even offer packages promising a certain amount of free liquor. For example, a recent *USA Today* article quoted the promotional literature of one packager as offering "50 hours of free drinking" in Mazatlan or Cancun. The student travel website StudentSpringBreak.com coos over "the luxurious beaches, the lush jungles, ancient ruins and the beautiful hotels" of Cancun, but concludes that "most students just care about the abundance of alcohol, alcohol and wait, you guessed it, more alcohol. Your yearly intake of alcoholic consumption could happen in one small week in Cancun, Mexico on Spring Break. Do I have to say more?" That website also promotes spring break in Europe, including Amsterdam, mentioning its museums and other cultural attractions, but specially highlighting the city's red-light district and the availability of legal pot.

Not unexpectedly, the U.S. Department of State takes a rather more sober view of international spring break. "Over 100,000 American teenagers and young adults travel to resort areas throughout Mexico over Spring Break each year," a State Department document notes. "While the vast majority enjoys their vacation without incident, several may die, hundreds will be arrested, and still more will make mistakes that could affect them for the rest of their lives."

Although U.S.-based websites may tout the liberal nature of Mexican law (as well as the laws of some other countries), it is crucial to remember that while traveling abroad you are subject to local laws—which, in many situations, are not nearly as liberal as advertised. "Mexican law can impose harsh penalties for violations that would be considered minor in the United States," the U.S. Department of State warns, "and U.S. citizenship in no way exempts one from full prosecution under the Mexican criminal justice system." Should you find yourself in legal trouble abroad, the first move is to contact the closest U.S. Consulate, U.S. consular agency, or the U.S. Embassy. Usually, a consular official can visit you in prison, and he or she may be able to provide you with a list of local lawyers. But if you think that American consular officials can get you out of a foreign jail, well, they can do no such thing.

Alcohol and Drugs South of the Border

Spring break packagers may tout the abundance of booze at Mexican resorts, together with the 18-year-old drinking age, but the fact is that Mexican authorities often come down hard on people—including American young people—who exhibit public drunkenness or who are involved in alcohol- or drug-related incidents and accidents. Such offenses as disturbing the peace, lewd or indecent behavior, littering, driving under the influence, drinking on the street or on public transportation, using public transportation without payment, or making obscene or insulting remarks are treated as serious criminal offenses by Mexican authorities. Importing, buying, possessing, or using drugs can bring penalties typically harsher than those imposed on first-time offenders in the United States. These include imprisonment—without bail—for as much as a year *before* trial. Conviction carries prison terms running into several years. And if 18-year-olds can drink in Mexico, 16-year-olds are tried as adults.

Safety and Security

Mexican resort communities cater to tourists, including a lot of U.S. citizens with high expectations for safety and security. Nevertheless, the levels of safety and security may not always approach those that prevail north of the border. Emergency and medical aid may not be as forthcoming or thorough. Stay alert. Be careful.

Heed warning flags used on beaches. On Mexican beaches, black or red flags indicate dangerous conditions and warn swimmers not to enter the water. The Pacific waters of Mexico are famous for their beauty as well as their powerful undertows and rough surf along the beaches at all times.

> **Bad Idea!**
>
> Carrying weapons into Mexico is a very bad idea. The nation imposes harsh penalties for bringing even a single bullet across its borders. In fact, it is inadvisable to carry anything that might by any stretch be construed as a weapon—such as a pocketknife.

In the city, use only the licensed, regulated, and clearly marked *sitio* (tourist) taxis. Unlicensed taxis are completely unregulated and may be operated by criminals in search of victims. Hotels, clubs, and restaurants will call a *sitio* taxi at your request.

Behind the Wheel

All drivers are subject to local laws. A U.S. driver's license is valid in most countries, including Mexico; however, Mexican law requires that vehicles be driven only by their owners (or renters) or that the owner (or renter) be inside the vehicle when it is being driven by someone else. The penalty for violating this law is permanent confiscation of the vehicle.

Before you drive into or within Mexico, review your insurance policy. You should have a full coverage policy that will cover the cost of bail. If you are involved in an automobile accident, the police will hold you until it is determined who is at fault and whether you have the ability to pay any penalty. Operators of any vehicle—car, scooter, jet ski, whatever—that causes damage to other vehicles or injuries to other people may be held in custody until full payment is made, either in cash or through insurance.

Advice from the U.S. Department of State

One of the responsibilities of the State Department is to advise U.S. citizens on potentially dangerous conditions in foreign countries. Here is what the department has to say about several popular spring break destinations in Mexico:

◆ **Acapulco.** Drug-related violence has been increasing in Acapulco. Although this violence is not targeted at foreign residents or tourists, U.S. citizens in these areas should be vigilant in their personal safety. Avoid swimming outside the bay area. Several American citizens have died while swimming in rough surf at the Revolcadero Beach near Acapulco.

◆ **Cabo San Lucas.** Beaches on the Pacific side of the Baja California Peninsula at Cabo San Lucas are dangerous due to rip tides and rogue waves; hazardous beaches in this area are clearly marked in English and Spanish.

◆ **Cancun and Cozumel.** Cancun is a fairly large city, approaching 500,000 inhabitants, with increasing reports of crime. Crimes against the person, such as rape, commonly but not exclusively occur at night or in the early morning hours, and often involve alcohol and the nightclub environment. Therefore, it is important to travel in pairs or groups, be aware of surroundings, and take general precautions. To protect against property crimes, valuables should be left in a safe place or not brought at all.

If you rent a moped or other vehicle in Cancun, it is advisable to purchase third-party insurance, as the insurance offered on some credit cards will not cover you in Mexico. Should you have an accident or cause damage to the vehicle, you may be required to pay the full amount of any repairs, in cash, as determined by the rental agency, or face arrest.

In Cancun, there is often a very strong undertow along the beach from the Hyatt Regency all the way south to Club Med. In 2006, several U.S. citizens drowned when overwhelmed by ocean conditions. In Cozumel, several drownings and near-drownings have been reported on the east coast, particularly in the Playa San Martin–Chen Rio area.

◆ **Matamoros/South Padre Island.** The Mexican border cities of Matamoros and Nuevo Progresso are located 30 to 45 minutes south of the major Spring Break destination of South Padre Island, Texas. Travelers to the Mexican border should be especially aware of safety and security concerns due to increased violence in recent years between rival drug trafficking gangs competing for control of narcotics smuggling routes. While it is unlikely that American visitors would get caught up in this violence, travelers should exercise commonsense precautions such as visiting only the well-traveled business and tourism areas of border towns during daylight and early-evening hours.

◆ **Mazatlan.** While the beach town of Mazatlan is a relatively safe place to visit, travelers should use common sense and exercise normal precautions when visiting an unfamiliar location. Avoid walking the streets alone after dark, when petty crimes are much more common. Beaches can have very strong undertows and rogue waves. Swimmers should obey warning signs placed along the beaches that indicate dangerous ocean conditions.

◆ **Nogales/Sonora.** Puerto Peñasco, a.k.a. "Rocky Point," is located in northern Sonora, 60 miles from the U.S. border, and is accessible by car. The majority of accidents that occur at this Spring Break destination are caused by individuals driving under the influence of alcohol. Travelers should exercise particular caution on unpaved roads, especially in beach areas.

◆ **Oaxaca City.** There have been ongoing demonstrations and protests in Oaxaca City due to civil unrest since June 2006. Several groups have engaged in violent demonstrations in Oaxaca City, which resulted in the death of an American citizen in October 2006. Prior to traveling to Oaxaca City, U.S. citizens should monitor the U.S. Embassy in Mexico City's website, http://mexico.usembassy.gov/mexico/citizen_services.html, as well as http://travel.state.gov for the most up-to-date safety and security information. U.S. citizens should avoid participating in demonstrations and other activities that might be deemed political by the Mexican authorities. The Mexican Constitution prohibits political activities by foreigners, and such actions may result in detention and/or deportation.

◆ **Oaxaca (coastal).** There have been a number of drownings along the beaches of the southern coast of Oaxaca, namely Zipolite Beach. Professional lifeguard training has contributed to a drop in fatalities, but swimmers are advised that currents can quickly become treacherous, even for accomplished swimmers.

◆ **Tijuana.** Tijuana has one of the busiest land border crossings in the world. The beach towns of Rosarito and Ensenada also attract a large number of tourists. Drinking alcoholic beverages excessively on a public street is prohibited.

Also according to the U.S. Department of State, Tijuana boasts a large number of pharmacies; to buy any controlled medication (e.g., Valium, Vicodin, Placidyl, Morphine, Demorol, and Ativan, etc.), a prescription from a Mexican federally registered physician is required. Possession of controlled medications without a Mexican doctor's prescription is a serious crime and can lead to arrest. The prescription must have a seal and serial number. Under no other circumstances should an individual purchase prescription medicines.

Register with the Embassy or Consulates

The U.S. Department of State recommends that all visitors to foreign countries register with the U.S. Embassy or Consulate. Doing so makes your presence and whereabouts known in case it's necessary for a consular officer to contact you in an emergency. You can register with the nearest U.S. Embassy or Consulate through the State Department's travel registration website.

Little Black Book

For the latest security information, Americans traveling abroad should regularly monitor the Department's Internet website at http://travel.state.gov. Here the current worldwide caution announcements, travel warnings, and other public announcements can be found. Up-to-date information on security can also be obtained by calling 1 888 407 4747 toll-free in the United States, or, for callers outside the United States and Canada, 202-501-4444. These numbers are available from 8 A.M. to 8 P.M. Eastern Time, Monday through Friday (except U.S. federal holidays).

The Roads Less Traveled

Many students think of spring break as a kind of rite of passage—or maybe just a right. After all, college is hard work with a lot of pressure, and all that earns you the *right* to party and act at least a little foolish.

Be aware that there are alternatives to the so-called "traditional" spring break blow-out. The majority of American college students do not go on special trips during spring break. Instead, they spend time with their families at home. Others, especially in law school, prelaw, and premed, use the time to study in informally organized groups. Still others plan more sedate vacations to places of special interest to them— perhaps backpacking in Yosemite, touring sites of special historical interest in New England, or visiting the art museums of Paris.

In recent years, more and more students have been dedicating their spring break time to charitable work, including aiding victims of natural disaster or people in financial need, through such organizations as Habitat for Humanity. Your college or university can provide you with ideas and contacts for genuinely rewarding alternative spring break experiences.

The Least You Need to Know

♦ Spring break is traditionally associated with the beach, the sun, drinking, sex, and generally high-risk behavior, prompting a number of communities to slam the door on vacationing students.

♦ The freewheeling aura of spring break notwithstanding, local laws apply—and may be enforced with particular vigor.

♦ Staying safe on spring break requires the same vigilance and common sense that help keep you safe in any other situation.

♦ Each year, many students fall victim to too-good-to-be-true spring break travel-package scams.

♦ Spending spring break abroad—especially in Mexico—has become an increasingly popular option. Be aware that local laws apply, as do local standards of police and medical services.

♦ Consider some rewarding alternatives to the traditional spring break.

Part 3

The People You Meet

Here you will find advice on avoiding and dealing with conflict, with special emphasis on how to prevent friction with your roommate from erupting into World War III. Also included is a chapter on dating without risking your physical or emotional health and on what to do when you encounter disturbing and possibly dangerous people.

Chapter 10

Conflict: Surviving Your Roommate—and Others

In This Chapter

♦ Avoiding—and managing—conflict

♦ How to focus on issucs instead of personalities

♦ Anger management

♦ The art of saying no

♦ When to ask for help—and when to call it quits

♦ Recognizing and dealing with emergencies

"Love and marriage," the old song goes, "go together like a horse and carriage." (I told you the song was old.) Ideally, you end up living with someone you love, someone you somehow feel that you were destined to be with: a soul mate. Of course, many marriages are very far from ideal, and many a husband or wife has awakened one morning, turned to his or her spouse asleep on the other pillow, and thought: "Who *is* this person?"

Well, since roommates are rarely soul mates—or were ever meant to be—it's not surprising that this question arises far more often among roommate "couples" than among married ones.

As in marriage, sometimes the answer leads to separation and divorce, preferably on amicable terms. But sometimes the only answer is to learn to live together—peacefully, productively, and safely. And if you can survive your roommate, you can deal safely and productively with all kinds of personal conflict on campus and off. Successfully negotiating life with a roommate is good practice for your postgraduate career, in which you have to work with all kinds of people.

An Ounce of Prevention

Whether the issue is sickness, accident, or conflict, prevention is always cheaper, easier, and more desirable than attempted cures and fixes. Depending on the rules and policies of your college or university, you may or may not have a choice in selecting your dormitory roommate. Even if you do have a choice, you may only have a certain degree of choice—typically the opportunity to say something about yourself and express your preferences on a housing questionnaire. Even if you are living off campus, in a shared apartment or house, your range of roommate choices may be limited or dictated by financial condition and availability rather than by perceived or proven compatibility or friendship.

At first thought, it may seem obvious: better to room with a friend than a stranger. But this is not necessarily the case. It's one thing to be someone's friend and quite another to live with him or her. Often, the longer and better you know someone, the more difficult it is to manage conflicts. A lot more emotions can get in the way. On the other hand, totally random roommate assignment may result in two fundamentally incompatible people being forced to share the same small space.

Speak Up, Listen Up

Is there any way to win?

While nothing you do can guarantee perfectly smooth relations with a roommate, you can take steps to significantly improve the odds.

Step one is to communicate. If you plan to room with a friend, have a long, frank conversation about the prospect before you commit. Talk about your expectations, your likes, and your dislikes. Identify possible areas of conflict and talk about how you plan to resolve them. Do at least as much listening as talking.

Even if your college does not permit you to choose your dorm roommate, chances are it does employ some sort of questionnaire system—typically this consists of an online form—that allows housing administrators to match up students who are likely to be compatible. Often, the system generates several potential matches from which you may choose persons to contact.

Fill out such forms carefully, thoughtfully, and—above all—honestly. You are creating a compatibility profile. You are presenting yourself and will not only have to live with the roommate the profile helps to attract, but you will have to live with yourself. Your object should not be to impress or to create a false impression, but to identify points of compatibility and possible conflicts.

> **Safe Move**
>
> Complete your survey questionnaire without delay. Turn it in well before the housing office deadline. This puts you into play early in the game, when there are a lot of people to match up. The housing staff therefore has a better chance of finding someone who appears to have the greatest degree of compatibility with you.

When you've identified potential roommates, contact them by phone or e-mail. Have a friendly but frank discussion, addressing expectations, likes and dislikes, possible areas of conflict. As you would if you were talking with a friend, be sure to do at least as much listening as talking.

Ease Up, Shut Up

In all the talking you do, avoid coming on too strong. Some things, doubtless, are very important to you, but surely some things are more important than others. Decide on areas of compromise, then be willing to compromise.

Know when to ease up and shut up. There is a fine line between making your preferences known and being dictatorial, unreasonable, and unpleasant. You may turn off and turn away a prospective roommate if you are harsh in your "demands" or, even worse, you may succeed in beating him or her into submission, only to have a simmering resentment erupt a month or so into the new semester.

The objective is give *and* take, not simply give *or* take.

Make Plans Together

If your college does the matching, you will be sent your roommate's contact information in advance of the start of the semester. Make contact right away. If this is in fact your first conversation, don't start laying down the law or looking for trouble. You may or may not be able to get a different roommate, but more than likely, you will have to learn to live with this person for at least a semester. Therefore, it's best to use your first contact to introduce yourselves and get to know one another. Start with easy, general questions:

- What made you choose XYZ College?
- Do you have a major?
- Are you into sports? Band? Computer games?
- What's your hometown like?
- What are you doing during the summer?
- Great talking with you. When should we talk again?

In that next conversation, zero in on some roommate-focused issues:

- What kind of music do you like?
- What do you do for fun?
- Are you a night person or a morning person?
- I've got a 17-inch LCD TV; do you have a portable refrigerator?
- Are you neat or sloppy?
- Do you have a boyfriend/girlfriend? Will he/she be visiting often?

Don't freak out about any of the answers you may get, but do use them to adjust your expectations and lay the groundwork for some ground rules.

If you're able to choose your roommate or roommates, it's a good idea to do some planning in advance. Even if you don't have a choice, it's quite possible that, at some time during the semester, issues may crop up that call for planning. In some schools, a certain degree of planning is actually required. The RA (resident advisor; see Chapter 3) may distribute (either on paper or online) formal "roommate agreements," which, really, are nothing more than a set of formalized plans—a working out and statement of mutual expectations.

Plan together with your roommate or roommates to establish expectations and rules concerning such hot-button issues as ...

Safe Move

Even if your school does not require a formal "roommate agreement" or "contract," consider putting down important rules in writing. If you create your own "contract," make sure that all roommates are involved in writing it and everyone agrees to it. Don't force a homemade contract on anyone.

- ◆ Privacy.

- ◆ Friend, boyfriend, and girl-friend visitation.

- ◆ Sleep and study schedules.

- ◆ Sharing and not sharing— of food, books, videos, CDs, MP3s, computers, even clothing.

- ◆ Rules for taking telephone messages.

Agreements can be very useful for identifying conflicts as they occur and working out their resolution.

Fix Problems, Not People

Before we go any further, some good news: the vast majority of roommate conflicts can be satisfactorily resolved. But we do need to add an if: *if* you always try to fix problems and never try to fix people.

The fact is that conflicts are sparked by particular issues—things people say or do—rather than by people themselves. What we call a "personality conflict" is really a conflict caused by particular items of behavior, including actions and words.

This is an important distinction and also a very fortunate one. It's fortunate because it's almost impossible to "fix" a person—to alter someone's personality—but often quite easy to "fix" a particular item of behavior, to change an action or a manner of expression.

Disagree Without Being Disagreeable

If you commit to fixing problems instead of people, you will find that you can disagree without having to become disagreeable. Nobody likes to be criticized, but if you and your roommate can separate the problem—the item of unpleasant behavior, the unpleasant words—from the person responsible for them, you can criticize the problem rather than the person.

History, sports, and many professions are full of fierce rivals who are nevertheless good personal friends. Two of today's most famous political consultants, Mary Matalan and James Carville, stand on opposite sides of the political fence—Matalan a conservative Republican and Carville a liberal Democrat—yet they are (at least to all appearances) very happily married. Do they have political arguments at home? They certainly do when they appear together on TV. So how do they stay together? They argue about politics, not about personalities. Maybe Carville tells Matalan, "I don't like your Republican stance on issue X," but he doesn't say, "I don't like you because you're a Republican."

Your roommate makes a habit of leaving ancient and decayed food items in the minifridge the two of you share. The result is a grotesque science project gone very wrong. You are tempted to explode: "John, I'm sick and tired of living with a pig!" Instead, you say: "John, please don't leave old food in the fridge. It's taking up room, and it really stinks."

The first approach attacks John as a person. The second does not address John at all, but focuses exclusively on the old, moldy food in the fridge. The first approach is likely to produce a defensive, offended, and angry response that may or may not incidentally result in a cleaner refrigerator.

The second approach is likely to produce calm compliance—"Sure. Sorry. I'll throw it out"—almost certainly resulting in exactly what you want: a tolerably clean refrigerator.

Now, think. Is the conflict about John's being a pig, or is it about disgusting old food in the refrigerator?

And think further. Almost certainly, your attempt to transform John from pig to neat freak will fail, but you probably *can* get him to remove his old food from the refrigerator—and he'll at least think twice before leaving a rotting burrito there again.

> ### Little Black Book
>
> *My Roommate Is Driving Me Crazy!* by Susan Fee (Adams Media, 2005) is a very helpful one-stop sourcebook of ideas for resolving common roommate problems and disputes.

Tackle the Issues

The vast majority of conflicts can be broken down to a particular action or word or set of actions or words that are at issue. In resolving the conflict, there's no need to leap over these words or actions to attack the person who is responsible for them. Stop at the issue *before* you reach the personality. You have a far, far better chance of fixing a problem than you do of fixing a person.

This said, don't let problems fester. Talk them out. Of course, people get angry and frustrated if you tell them they're bad or stupid or sloppy or selfish or deficient in some way. It's not just because criticizing someone's character or personality is inherently offensive, it's also because such criticism is useless. It's like telling a short person that you would like him better if he were tall. At the very least, it's not helpful.

Attack: "Stop being a pig."

Response: "I'm sloppy. That's my nature. I can't change. *You* are a neat freak. That's your nature. *You* can't change."

Such exchanges get nowhere—or, at least, nowhere you want to be. However, if you identify a particular issue and suggest a way of addressing it, you not only avoid insulting the other person, you give him a helping hand: "John, please don't leave old food in the fridge. It's taking up room, and it really stinks." You've identified a problem and supplied a solution. No offense has been given, and no frustration created. You aren't asking John to change his personality, just to stop leaving old junk in the fridge.

Bad Idea!

It's always a bad idea to demand a transformation of personality. First, it will never happen. Second, it will create frustration and anger. On the other hand, define a problem and then suggest a solution, and the other person will probably be pleased to comply with your request. We all like to be successful, and pleasing others is a sign of success.

Calm Down

One of the big advantages of the fix-problems-not-people approach is that it often prevents a conflict from escalating into a shouting match—or worse—and, in fact, it even gets the problem resolved. The approach does require adhering to some ground rules:

1. Define a problem that can be solved, and solved reasonably and fairly. Ask John to take his old food out of the refrigerator, but don't insist that he clean out the whole refrigerator. (However, you might suggest that the two of you pitch in together to clean out the fridge. "It'll take us about three minutes.")

Bad Idea!

Usually, telling an angry person to "calm down" only produces greater anger. Instead, let your roommate vent. Resist the impulse to holler back in return. After he or she has vented, try to turn the discussion away from personalities and focus it back on issues.

2. Do not bury the other person under a laundry list of problems: "... and another thing ... and, besides that ..., and that's not even the worst of it ...." This is overwhelming. Not only is it likely to frustrate your roommate and thereby provoke an angry response, it will probably get you worked up as well as you spew forth your list. Define and address one or two issues at a time. Be patient.

3. Do not add judgments on morals, character, or personality. "John, only pigs leave old food to rot in the fridge."

4. It's all right to let your roommate know that something he or she does or says upsets you, but state this factually. Do not vent your anger. Stay calm.

5. If you're really upset, calm down before you talk to your roommate. Remember, conflict resolution is about solving specific problems, not about venting your emotions.

Walk Away

Keeping the conversation focused on issues—behaviors to be changed, problems to be solved—instead of personalities goes a long way toward keeping the conversation rational, civil, and productive. But let's not kid ourselves. It doesn't always work.

If the discussion becomes heated, suggest a break: "John, we're both getting worked up. Let's take a break and talk about this a little later, okay? I'm going to the gym." Or: "John, this is getting us nowhere. Do you want to take a break and talk about this later? No use getting all worked up."

Don't just stalk off with a harsh word or a silent stare. Nevertheless, it is better to walk away than to get into a heated argument. Walking away is a temporary measure, a safety valve. It's also something you can agree on: "Yes, Tom. I need to go to the library anyway. Let's both cool off and figure this thing out."

Say No—Without Slamming the Door

Here's a blinding flash of the obvious: conflict rarely follows *yes*, but often follows *no*. In other words, conflict is not the product of agreement, but disagreement.

Obviously. But does that mean you always have to say yes—that you have to agree—in order to avoid conflict?

It does not. For one thing, in order to have your own life, you need to retain the right to say no to any number of things. For another, if conflict often flows from saying no, it is also the result of saying yes when you really mean no.

The best way to avoid conflict is to say no when you mean no, but to say no without slamming the door behind you. Say no to some*thing*, not some*one*. For instance:

Question: "Can I borrow your car this afternoon?"

Answer: "I'm not letting you drive my car."

This is saying no to the person, not the request. Instead, refocus the no on the request:

"John, I promised my dad that I would not let anyone else drive the car. He's paying for the insurance."

Many of us find it hard to say no, and even more of us find it hard to say no without slamming the door. Here are some guidelines for saying no without creating conflict:

- ◆ Don't say yes when you really mean no.

- ◆ If you find that you often want to say no, but somehow always end up saying yes instead, get into the habit of taking a deep breath and holding it for a three count before responding. This will help interrupt your reflexive "yes" response and give you the few seconds you need to think of a way to say no.

- ◆ "No" often triggers conflict because it frustrates the person on the receiving end, making him feel powerless. The antidote to this reaction is the offer of alternatives that empower the person to whom you are saying no. "John, I can't do X, but I can do Y or Z."

- ◆ Before you say no, think about self-interest—not *your* self-interest, but the other person's. Persuade her that "no" is not just *your* response, but the right answer for *her*. You are asked for the loan of $25. Instead of exploding that your roommate already owes you $20, focus on why lending another $25 is a bad idea—*for her*. "Ann, you've owed me $20 for a month now. I'm not going to add to your debt."

- ◆ Don't say yes when you mean no, but don't let no become a knee-jerk response. Look for an alternative to a simple yes or no. Instead of saying no, compromise on a favorable solution. The classic alternative to no is a quid pro quo: "If you lend me your physics notes, I'll help you with Spanish." A demonstration of flexibility often wins the day, whereas a flat no may bring about mutually defeating confrontation.

◆ As far as you can, plan any confrontation thoroughly. Know what you want, anticipate potential objections, formulate responses. This does not mean burning the word "no" into your mind, but it does mean having any relevant facts and arguments ready so that you can trot them out as required.

◆ If possible, avoid saying no and leaving it at that. Try a *feel-felt-found* approach. It builds a bridge of empathy and understanding that helps both of you get over the feelings of having been thwarted: "I know how you *feel* ... I *felt* that way myself once ... But I have *found* that ...."

◆ Say no, but don't say "hell, no." It's better to underreact than to overreact. Emotions feed off one another. The word "no" can create powerful, usually negative, feelings. Don't stoke the fires of resentment by upping the emotional ante with a loud voice or harsh words.

Seek Mediation

If you find yourself running up against a wall every time you try to work things out with your roommate—or with anyone else, for that matter—consider seeking mediation from an objective third party.

In some situations, both inside and outside the dorm, bringing in a mutual friend can help, although such a mediator always risks losing one or more friendships. In the dorm, if you honestly feel that you have exhausted all of your options—if you've thoroughly discussed your concerns with your roommate, if you have tried to work things out, if you have talked and listened—take it to the next level. Call on the RA. Mediating disputes is one of her principal jobs.

In a dorm situation, bringing in the RA can be a tough judgment call. However, if your roommate is doing anything illegal or dangerous—anything that you believe jeopardizes your safety—talk to the RA immediately.

Be completely open and honest with the RA. Explain the conflict, and explain what you and your roommate have done in an effort to resolve it. If the RA judges that the conflict is a manageable one, she will act as a moderator while the two of you talk it out. Yes, you've been over this ground before, but in the presence of an objective moderator, the two of you may see a solution.

Bad Idea!

> Unless you feel that you're in danger, don't go to the RA without telling your roommate that you are doing so. It will appear to him that you are going behind his back or that you are "reporting" him. Creating either impression is a bad idea. Don't use the RA as a threat, but do let your roommate know that you want to consult him: "Look, John, I think it's time to go to the RA."

If the conflict is more serious, the RA may recommend that either you, your roommate, or the two of you together consult a campus counseling service (see Chapter 14). Don't be offended or alarmed. Follow the RA's advice. Campus counseling is confidential, and it may well serve to give you a fresh and helpful perspective on your problem.

Calling It Quits

You have an investment in the people who are most important to you: friends, family, girlfriends, boyfriends. Naturally, when conflict develops with these people, you want to take the time and make the effort to reach a happy resolution. Your relationship is simply more important than the conflict.

Sometimes roommates become good friends. Sometimes they don't. Even when a roommate is only a roommate, you owe him or her respect and consideration. In a conflict, you owe each other the time and effort to reach a productive, satisfactory, and safe resolution. Yet the fact is that some differences are—as the divorce courts say—irreconcilable.

If you (and, even more, if both you and your roommate) believe that your differences are irreconcilable, do not get angry or angrier with each other. First talk to the RA, then to the dorm or hall director (if there is one), and then to the appropriate authority in the university's housing office. Every residential college and university has a policy and a procedure for room changes. Usually, your RA is the best source for finding out what these policies and procedures are.

If you and your roommate agree that you need a room change, the process will be easier. If you can readily agree on who should do the moving, it's easier still. Moreover, if multiple roommates are involved, everyone will have to come to an agreement.

If you and your roommate or roommates cannot reach a decision on who does the moving, then the housing office will have to decide what's fair—and all of you will have to live with that decision. However, the housing office cannot work miracles. Residence halls may well be filled to capacity, especially in the fall semester. In this case, you and your roommate may have to work together to find another pair of room-mates who want to split up. Then you can swap with them. Of course, the difficulty here is that you and your roommate have found it difficult or impossible to cooperate with one another—that's why you want to change rooms!—and yet you must now cooperate to find a pair willing to swap with you.

Working with a difficult person can be just as hard as living with one; however, if you have decided that you need a change, cooperation is your only alternative to misery, stress, and continued conflict, which may escalate into something both of you will regret.

"That Girl Has a *Serious* Problem"

Chapters 13 and 14 in this book deal with critical situations, including crises and emergencies involving physical and mental health and how to get immediate help. If the behavior, the actions, the words, the appearance, even the general demeanor of a friend, acquaintance, or roommate set off alarm bells inside you, take action.

Keep two facts uppermost in mind. First: each of us is ultimately responsible for our own physical and emotional health, including seeking help and treatment when necessary. You should care about your friend or roommate, but you are not and cannot be that person's parent or guardian. Second: never play doctor. Encourage your friend or roommate to talk to you, and listen to his or her problem, but don't offer a diagnosis. Never dismiss his or her complaint with "Oh, you'll snap out of it," or amplify it with, "My God, this sounds serious!" Listen and empathize, but suggest that the person consult campus counseling or go to student health.

Although it's not your job to play doctor—even if you're pre-med or a psych major—do not turn your back on symptoms of depression, anxiety, eating disorders, self-injury, substance abuse, threats of suicide, or other bizarre or disturbing behavior.

"I'm Just Going to Kill Myself ..."

We'll discuss in greater detail the most common emotional problems and emergencies encountered on campus in Chapter 13. There is one emergency, however, that needs to be hashed out here and now: the threat of suicide.

If your roommate or anyone else talks about committing suicide, even in what you think is a half-joking way, take it as a serious threat. Not everyone who commits suicide announces their intentions, but many do. They are, in fact, asking for help, for someone to intervene.

If your roommate or anyone else threatens suicide, stay with him or her. Talk. Do not leave the person alone. Contrary to what you may have heard, talking about suicide or depression will not make things worse. Talking about suicide will not plant the thought in the other person's mind (it's already planted, sprouted, and growing) or in any way prompt the action.

Your main job is to be there and to listen. You aren't expected to have any magic answers, and don't tell the person that everything will be all right or that what they're feeling is "nothing," or that they "really don't mean" what they say.

Do ask the person if he or she has taken any pills or anything else. If the answer is yes, dial 911 immediately. Even if the answer is no or noncommittal, if the person seems drugged, drowsy, confused, or out of it, assume that he or she has taken something. Call 911. Better a false alarm than a real tragedy.

Ask if there is any suicide plan. The question is simple: "How do you plan to kill yourself?" The more specific the answer you receive, the more serious and imminent the threat.

Report any suicidal behavior (including severe depression) or suicidal conversation to the closest available authority. In the dorm, this may be the RA or an assistant RA. If he or she is unavailable, call the campus suicide crisis line (if your campus has one), the counseling center, or student health. If you cannot get hold of anyone immediately, call campus security or 911. Explain the situation.

Safe Move

If the crisis has escalated beyond the talking phase, if it looks to you as if the person is in immediate danger of harming himself or others, call 911 immediately.

"I Don't Want to Talk About It"

Not everyone who is hurting asks for help. If the behavior of your roommate—or anyone else close to you—is disturbing and, you fear, harmful to the person, to you, or to others, try to talk about it. If he or she refuses, let someone else in on the problem. In the dorm, the RA is a good first choice, but any of the other campus helpers are also likely candidates, including a counselor or someone at student health (see Chapter 14). Remember, what your friend or roommate does or does not do is ultimately his or her responsibility, but if you can help—especially by finding appropriate professional help—you need to do what you can, even if the other person asks you to leave them alone.

Unless you feel that the situation is an emergency (in which case, call 911 now), try—gently—to get the other person to open up to you before you ask others for help. Explain why you want him or her to open up:

♦ "I understand you don't think anything is wrong, but I have to tell you honestly, you seem like you are hurting."

♦ "I don't mean to upset you, and I don't want to make you angry—but I really hate to see you this way."

♦ "The only reason I'm bringing this up is because I care about you, and I want you to know that I'm here if you want to talk."

♦ "I'm sorry my asking you about this gets you angry, but I'm concerned about your safety."

Once you get your friend or roommate to talk to you, suggest that he or she talk to a counselor or, if you believe it's appropriate to the other person's beliefs, a campus chaplain. If you sense immediate danger—or if the other person has taken drugs (of any kind) or alcohol—call 911. When you are confronted with a roommate or friend in crisis, the only wrong move is no move at all. The only mistake you can make is to ignore what you see, hear, and feel.

The Least You Need to Know

- Conflict is inevitable in most relationships, but serious conflict can often be avoided and all conflict managed.

- The golden rule in resolving conflict is to focus on resolving specific problems rather than attempting to "fix" other people; tackle issues, do not attack personalities.

- Learning to say no when you mean no—yet without alienating anyone in the process—goes a long way to avoiding as well as resolving conflict.

- Know when to ask for help and who to ask.

- Never ignore crises of physical or emotional health, especially threats of suicide or suicidal behavior; always treat these as emergencies.

Chapter 11

Dating

In This Chapter

- ◆ "Rules" for safe dating
- ◆ Think with your brain instead of your heart
- ◆ The safest sex
- ◆ Date rape *is* rape
- ◆ Online dating precautions
- ◆ "No" means no

Look carefully at the title of this chapter. It might be one of the last times you'll see the word. These days, fewer college students speak of "dating." They don't like to use a word that implies people pairing up in what amounts to a more-or-less short-term rehearsal for long-term monogamy. In recent years, the more common pattern tends to be either a series of brief relationships or the formation of a "couple" consisting of two people who have known each other for a sustained period of time, though without formally dating.

So let's agree from the outset that by "dating" we mean any relationship, no matter how fleeting or how enduring, that includes a romantic or sexual dimension or, at least, the potential for one.

The Rules

People sometimes talk about "rules" for dating. Maybe these rules actually exist—somewhere—or maybe they are part of that vast, vague pool of illusory "knowledge" known as urban legend. It doesn't really matter, because, for all practical purposes, the only valid "rules" of dating are those you establish for yourself to make you comfortable in your social and romantic life. That said, while the rules of dating are personal and subjective, there are some rules of safety—which go along with dating—that should guide everyone.

Make a Plan

How can you *plan* romance, much less sexual attraction? Such things are, after all, compounded mostly of emotional spontaneity and biological urges.

True enough. You cannot plan your feelings or how others will feel about you, but you can plan the events, activities, occasions, and places in which you want to get together with another person—the venue in which all these feelings will play out. In other words, you can plan a date.

In any venture into the unknown, it's always better to have some sort of plan than to rely on a wing and a prayer. Even if the plan doesn't go as you expected—and it's likely that it won't—at least you'll have some idea of where you thought you wanted to go, so that you can adjust the direction of where you are actually going.

Decide in advance what you are comfortable doing. Know your physical and emotional boundaries. Make an exit plan part of your overall plan. Another component of any sound dating plan is to avoid blind dates—that is, solo dates with total strangers—and never go anywhere so remote that your ride back depends on how compliant you are with the quite possibly unwanted advances of your date.

A Place to Date

Part of your plan should include the venue for your date. You and the other person need to agree on where you are going. The safest dating opportunities are found on or near campus, which puts you and your date on an equal footing, giving both a home court advantage.

Consider going to a sporting event, seeing a movie on campus or at a theater close by, visiting a campus art show or attending a campus musical event, even meeting at the library to study together. Such venues have the advantage of being local, familiar, and more or less public. The time for intimacy will come later, after you have gotten to know each other. It's a good idea to see how a person behaves around others before you are alone with him or her.

As you get more comfortable with one another, consider such dating venues as a local club, an off-campus restaurant for dinner, or a visit to a local attraction (zoo, museum, amusement park).

Bad Idea!

Don't get lulled into a false sense of security just because you are on campus. Many campuses are big places where bad things can happen. For example, a frat house may be on campus, but it is not a good place for a first date with someone you hardly know.

Alone Together

As you become increasingly familiar and comfortable with someone, you will want to spend time in less public places, including time alone together. Until you reach this point of comfort in the relationship, observe the following rules. They are not *dating* rules, but *safety* rules founded firmly on common sense:

- ◆ Until you get to know the other person well—and are comfortable with him or her—stay in public places.

- ◆ Until you get to know the other person well, meet at the agreed-on date location. Do not ride in a stranger's car.

- ◆ When you go out on a date, tell a friend where you are going and with whom.

- ◆ Take your fully charged cell phone with you.

- ◆ Always have your own means of getting home or back to campus. Carry enough money for a taxi or other means of transportation.

◆ Even if you are old enough to drink, avoid drinking alcohol with anyone you do not know well.

Here's another rule. It's a safety rule, first and foremost, but it's also a good rule in any situation that involves you and another person: *never do anything that makes you feel uncomfortable.*

Your Objective?

Decide on your objective for this date. Some young men and young women believe that the objective of any date is sex. The "success" or "failure" of a date is determined by whether or not it ends with sex.

Safe Move

Now is a good time to review "Sexual Assault and Rape" in Chapter 4.

That is a personal choice. Some chess players will tell you that the objective of a game is to checkmate your opponent, whereas others insist that the only valid objective is to play a good game, win, lose, or draw. The latter are almost always the better players.

There is no law of dating that sets sex as the objective of the event. You are free to set any objective you wish. Want a suggestion? At minimum, set this as your objective: ending the date without having done anything that makes you feel uncomfortable. Add to this a second, third, and fourth objective: getting to know another person, enjoying his or her company, and having a good time wherever and however you *both* choose.

You may have one or more dating objectives in mind, and your date may have one or more in mind as well. Do you have the same objectives? Maybe. Maybe not. Find out. Talk about where you want to go and what you want to do. Come to an agreement.

As for the issue of sex, we'll talk more about it in a few moments.

Great Expectations

Whereas some people mistakenly identify sex as the only possible measure of a successful date, others make the even bigger mistake of defining a successful date as the start of a lifelong relationship.

This is asking an awful lot of a day at the amusement park or an evening at the movies. Whatever else a date may be, it's a social event, an opportunity to get to know someone and for that person to get to know you. Plan for this opportunity to take place safely and in an environment in which you and the other person are both comfortable. If you like each other enough to want to make another date, fine. If not, so be it. Either way, you have learned something about yourself and someone else. A date need go no further than this to be counted successful.

Ask! (and Answer)

How do you ask someone out on a date? You probably already know the answer. Just ask. The so-called rule dictating that the boy always asks the girl was broken, smashed, and shattered a long time ago. Male or female, if you are interested in someone, ask.

If the answer is no, do not persist. Get used to the idea that no means no. It means no at any point in a relationship, including before there even is any relationship. If you ask someone out on a date, and he or she says no, it ends there. If you are dating, and your bid to take the relationship to a more intimate level is met with no, it means no.

If you are the one who must answer the dating question, say yes if you mean yes, and say no if you mean no. Maybe you are afraid that saying no will hurt the other person's feelings. Well, it might. But it is far more hurtful to say yes—or to deliver a vague maybe—when you really mean no.

Bad Idea!

Don't assume that no somehow really means yes or even maybe. Forget anything you may have heard about someone "playing hard to get." No means no. Failure to understand this will, at the very least, create bad feelings; at worst, it may end in a criminal charge of sexual assault or rape against you.

Speaking from your true feelings is always the best—and safest—move. Be honest and straightforward. Playing hard to get is not alluring or sexy or attractive in any way. It is dishonest, and trying to build a relationship on dishonesty is like trying to build a house on sand. At the very least, it makes for instability; at worst, it sets up a dangerous situation.

Set Up a First Meeting Instead of a First Date

We've made some suggestions about setting up a "safe" first date. We've also mentioned that, these days, many people are uncomfortable with the whole idea of dating. Consider an alternative way of getting to know another person. Don't ask for a date; just set up a meeting.

What's the difference between a meeting and a date? The short answer is that a meeting has a set or implied time limit. It is for coffee or lunch or other daytime occasion of limited duration. It is less a romantic than a social occasion. As such, how the other person responds to your suggestion for a "meeting" will tell you much about him or her. If the other person agrees enthusiastically, that's a good indication that he or she is, above all, interested in you and getting to know you, under whatever circumstances. If the response is less than enthusiastic, the indication is strong that the other person will settle for nothing less than a date and is therefore less interested in getting to know you than in having someone to take to a movie or a club.

The great thing about setting up a first meeting instead of a first date is that a meeting eliminates certain expectations and therefore removes a good deal of emotional pressure. For many people, a date implies the expectation of romance or sex, whereas a simple meeting does not. This said, it must be noted that no law—or dating rule—states that saying yes to a date is also an agreement to romance or sex. If you are doing the asking, bear this in mind. If you are making the answer, be aware that you have not given up the absolute right to say no—no to a destination, no to an activity, no to a kiss, no to another date, and no to sex. And you may say no to any of these things in any order or combination.

Keep Your Eyes—and Your Mind—Open

Love at first sight is a wonderful thing. But we have to call it a "thing," because it's difficult to say just what it is in any particular instance. For some, love at first sight is an ideal, for others a myth, for some others a profound emotional and physical experience, and for still others it may simply be a biological urge.

You can save yourself a lot of trouble by trying to think with your brain instead of your heart. Open up your eyes, ears, and mind. Don't just focus on your own strong feelings, but continue to absorb what's happening around you. Take in how the other person treats you and those around you. Does he or she demonstrate concern for you and your feelings? Or is he or she self-centered? Is he or she courteous and friendly to others while also being charming to you? Or is he or she trying to monopolize you and your time, to consume you?

You may tell yourself that your charms make you irresistible, compelling the other person to be so possessive. Charming you may well be, but the truth about people who are noticeably possessive is that they were like that with the last person they were with and will be the same way with the next.

Don't stop feeling. But don't stop thinking, either. Whatever else a date is, it is an audition for a potential relationship. If you are treated or talked to thoughtlessly, selfishly, rudely, or manipulatively in the course of a meeting or a date, ask yourself: Do I want to multiply this behavior over the next several days, weeks, or months? People are generally on their best behavior on a date, so if you sense the seeds of physical or emotional abuse, count on it getting worse as dating develops into a relationship over time. Be especially wary of possessiveness—the sense that the other person does not let you be you. This may well develop into a stalking relationship, one in which the other person simply will not leave you alone, even after you have called it quits.

Safe Sex

Face it, sex can be risky. There is the danger of disease, unwanted pregnancy, abuse, and emotional pain. What is the safest "safe sex"? No sex at all. Abstinence is the safest sexual choice you can make.

That doesn't necessarily mean that it's the best choice for you, but it is a choice you should consider. Abstinence will protect you 100 percent from sexually transmitted diseases (STDs), unwanted pregnancies, and some possibly dangerous situations.

Making the Choice

If you do choose to have sex, take steps to protect yourself, both physically and emotionally.

Physically, it is critically important that a man uses a condom. Except for abstinence, condoms provide the greatest degree of protection from STDs, including HIV-AIDS, syphilis, gonorrhea, genital herpes, and other infections. If you or your partner do not have a condom, do not have sex. No one is immune from STDs, the effects of which range from miserable to fatal.

Condoms are also a highly effective birth-control measure, although it's always best to combine the use of a condom with some other form of birth control. Talk to your doctor or visit student health. Many colleges and university student health services offer birth control counseling.

Safe Move

Sex is a popular topic for conversation among friends. And it should be. The more you talk to friends about their beliefs, values, and experience, the more readily you will be able to discover your own values and feelings. Take a nonjudgmental approach. Defining and maintaining your own values never requires you to condemn the values of another.

For your emotional as well as physical well-being, define limits for yourself. There is no "right" way to have sex. Decide what type of sexual contact or sexual activity you want to have. If something makes you uncomfortable, physically or emotionally, if you don't want to do something, make this clear early in the sexual encounter. No one has the right to criticize you as uptight or inhibited. Where sex is concerned, no one has the right to push you beyond your physical, emotional, or moral comfort zone.

Decide for yourself how long you need to know your partner before you have sex with him or her. Again, there are no set rules about this. But you need to sort out for yourself your own thoughts and values. How well do you need to know the other person? And what, exactly, do you need to know about him or her?

Talk It Out

Myth: talking about "safe sex" as well as other sexual likes and dislikes is a turn-off. We human beings may be animals, but we're social
and moral animals. Sex requires accepting responsibility, and because
two people are involved, two people must share the responsibility. If
you cannot talk freely, openly, and productively with your partner
about safe sex as well as all other aspects of sex, then you are both well
advised not to add this dimension to your relationship until you can
talk about these things. Remember, too, that safe sex, including birth
control, is the responsibility of both partners in a sexual relationship.

Date Rape

Rape is nonconsensual—not agreed upon—sex. It's when one person
forces another person to have sex against his or her will, sometimes by
means of violence or the threat of violence. In some cases, the victim is
under the influence of alcohol or drugs.

Date rape is rape. It is nonconsensual sex in which one person forces
another person to have sex. The only difference between rape and date
rape is that, in the case of date rape, the victim has agreed to spend
time with the attacker. The victim may have even spent time with the
attacker on more than one occasion. In the eyes of the law, none of this
matters. Date rape is rape, a felony.

If you say no to sex and sex is forced on you, you have been raped.

If the person you are dating says no to your sexual advances, and you
force that person to have sex anyway, you are guilty of rape.

Rape, including date rape, is not limited to intercourse in the vagina.
Intercourse in the mouth or anus is also considered rape under law
and is a felony offense. Other forms of sexual contact may be judged as
sexual assault, also a felony, even in the context of a date.

If you are the victim of date rape, take the same actions that you would
take if you had been raped by a stranger. Do not wash or douche. It is
important that you do not wash away any evidence that could be used
against your attacker in court.

> **Little Black Book**
>
> If your school has one, the campus rape crisis center is probably your best resource for rape counseling. Most cities and even smaller towns also maintain rape counseling centers. You can also contact the Suicide and Rape 24-Hour Emergency Services National Hotline at 1-800-333-4444.

Call the police and report what happened. You should not be afraid to call the police, but, if you are, call the campus rape crisis center or your local rape crisis center.

Go to an emergency room, where you will be examined. A health care provider will make a record of any injuries and will treat you. At this time, samples of any fluid left in the vagina or anus will be collected, as will hair and other trace evidence left by the attacker.

Rape—especially date rape—often creates guilty feelings in the victim. You should get counseling for yourself as soon as possible.

Dating Online

So-called "online dating" is not really dating so much as it is using online chat rooms or dedicated online dating services to meet someone you might like to date. We've covered the safety and security concerns of online dating in Chapter 6, but we need to state here a version of what we've said earlier about the safest "safe sex."

Just as the only truly safe sex is no sex, so the only truly safe online dating is no online dating. As Chapter 6 explains, there are many things you can do to reduce the risks of online dating, but that does not change the fact that no place is more frequented by sexual predators, child molesters, deviants, and other undesirables than the Internet. Whatever else the Internet has given us—and it has given us much—it has also provided a more or less socially acceptable outlet for those who formerly stayed by themselves, reading pornography while wishing something like the Internet would be invented.

The principal risk of online communication is that you really have no idea with whom you are communicating. You may believe you are chatting with an attractive woman in her 20s when, in reality, the other party is a twisted cross-dressing sexual offender. That sensible college student from a neighboring state may actually be a high-school dropout recently released from prison.

If you do decide to try meeting someone online, review Chapter 6. Make certain you do not give out any personal information. Do not put your photo online. Do not tell anyone where you live or what kind of car you drive. Don't be political or identifiable in any way. Such practices as listing your social calendar on Facebook, MySpace, or the like is particularly risky. No website can be so secure that only 100 percent upstanding citizens are allowed to participate. Stalkers and predators use these and other websites to prey on victims.

Choose not to be a victim. You can tell the truth while still guarding your identity. You have no obligation to identify yourself to those you don't know. Never divulge information by which a predator can track you down.

If you do decide to meet someone IRL ("in real life") you've connected with online, don't go to the meeting alone. Take a friend, and meet in public—a restaurant or coffee shop is a good idea.

Bad Idea!

It is not safe to meet an online contact at a shopping mall, particularly if the person suggests that you do. Malls are the classic territory of online predators. You are playing on their field, because they have scoped out the territory thoroughly and are intimately familiar with ways to get you to let down your guard. You may be plied with gifts or money, and, before you know it, you may find yourself in the clutches of someone from who you cannot easily escape.

Drinking and Dating

We've discussed alcohol and drugs in Chapter 8. Since both drink and drugs generally reduce our natural inhibitions, they have long been used in dating situations as social and sexual lubricants. Sometimes both dating partners decide to get buzzed. Sometimes one will work hard to get the other drunk.

Drinking or smoking marijuana clouds your ability to see danger. These substances may also tend to turn a frog into a prince and a dog into a princess. But who wants to look at the world through beer-colored glasses? You can't be drunk all the time.

Drinking alcohol or using other substances on a date, especially a date before you know the other person, is risky business. If you are of legal age and you decide to drink, be sure you are in a setting where you will be safe and will not be at the mercy of someone who may not have your safety as his or her primary interest.

Hard Fact

So-called "date rape" drugs are all too real. Benzodiazepines, especially Rohypnol (the street name is "roofie"), can incapacitate victims and prevent them from resisting sexual assault (see "Being There" in Chapter 9). The drug can also produce anterograde amnesia, which means that the victim may not remember events they experienced while under the effects of the drug. Roofies are typically dissolved in alcoholic beverages. Never leave your drink unattended at the bar. If the drink looks strange (especially if it is cloudy) or tastes strange, do not drink it.

It should go without saying—but we must say it anyway—that drinking and driving never mix. And maybe that's a good reason for you to do the driving on a first date. Not only does that put you in greater control of your destiny—you can leave whenever you want—it also gives you a supremely good reason not to drink.

The Meaning of No

Let's end by repeating the most important word either partner can utter on a date. That word is *no*. Whatever else you forget when you are with another person, always remember that no means no.

Be firm when you say no. Don't say no unless you mean no. Don't say no when you really mean yes, and don't say yes or maybe when you really mean no. Use no without ambiguity.

If you are on the receiving end of no, take it at face value and for what it is: your final answer.

The Least You Need to Know

◆ There is no rulebook for dating, but common sense will help you to formulate and follow rules for safe dating.

◆ The best place for a first date is somewhere public. Don't go off alone together until you know one another well.

◆ Saying yes to a date does not obligate you to say yes to sex—or anything else, for that matter.

◆ The safest "safe sex" is no sex—abstinence—but if you choose to have sex, practice safe sex by using a condom and by setting limits with which you are comfortable.

◆ Date rape is nonconsensual sex between two people who know one another. Even if it is not violent, it is still rape—a crime.

◆ Be honest with the other person. When you mean no, say no. When you mean yes, say yes.

Chapter 12

Disturbing People, Dangerous People

In This Chapter

- ◆ Never ignore disturbing or dangerous behavior
- ◆ Drawing the line between diversity and deviance
- ◆ Reading the warning signs
- ◆ When to call the cops

He was a student some described as "brooding." He never took his sunglasses off. Those who *encountered* him—nobody claimed really to *know* him—said he was always angry or menacing or disturbed. Sometimes he seemed so depressed that it appeared he was about to cry. When he spoke, it was typically in a whisper, but mostly, he remained silent. In a creative writing class, he spent time taking photographs of fellow students, yet he never looked directly at any of them. Often, he wore his iPod earphones, even in class. When he wrote, he wrote almost exclusively about death. Students in the creative writing class became so unnerved by his presence that many stopped coming to class.

His creative writing professor was sufficiently troubled by how he acted, what he wrote, and the effect he had on other students that she spoke to her department chairman, who in turn interviewed the student and urged him to seek counseling, even offering to walk him to the counseling center. He replied that he would think about it. After he left her office, the department chairman warned school officials about the young man's strange behavior. The officials were sympathetic, but because the student had made no actual threats, they said that there was little they could do.

The young man was Cho Seung Hui, who, at Virginia Tech in Blacksburg, Virginia, on April 16, 2007, shot and killed 32 students, wounded 21 others, then killed himself.

Diversity or Deviance?

Almost every campus takes pride in being open, accepting, and welcoming of diversity of every kind—religious, ethnic, racial, cultural, intellectual, emotional. Tolerance and openness are essential to free inquiry, the very foundation of a liberal education. Sadly, however, there is a downside to this attitude when it takes the rigid form of political correctness, in which common sense is stifled and a blind eye is deliberately turned to some things—some differences—that should matter.

There was a time when a loner who did not speak to his roommates, had an imaginary girlfriend, and often said or wrote disturbing things, would be challenged for his behavior rather than "accepted," which—let's face it—is just another word for ignored.

A college campus is a community whose members have a responsibility to protect themselves. Some actions and some behavior are just not normal. Even so, most of these actions and behaviors are not particularly disturbing, let alone alarming. We tolerate them, especially in the tolerant atmosphere of campus. But some actions and some behavior are so far from normal that they cannot be excused as mere idiosyncrasies.

When you encounter someone who presents a disturbing picture—who avoids others, who talks of death and killing, who in some way seems far beyond the range of normal—it is perfectly appropriate for you to raise your guard.

You don't have to be rude, just careful. You don't have to run away, but you might want to stay out of the way. Few moves are safer than listening to your intuition. And intuition is a very real thing. It is your contact with a set of primal senses that help to keep you alive.

If someone "feels" like trouble, act on your feeling. That certainly doesn't mean picking a fight, pointing a finger, or starting a rumor. It means being watchful and staying out of that person's way. It means taking responsibility for your safety.

Safe Move

Watching out for yourself and your campus community isn't rocket science, nor does it require a Ph.D. in psychology. Stay attuned to behavior that is distinctly out of place. Also watch for people who just don't belong. This isn't always easy on big campuses or urban campuses, but even on a large campus, you soon get an idea of who has legitimate business on campus and who may not. If you see a stranger roaming campus or loitering, do not challenge him or her. Notify the campus police right away. Give your location and describe the person.

A Fine Line

There is a line to be drawn in our society between diversity and deviance, and sometimes that line is a very fine one. It's common to encounter young people with purple hair, piercings (in visible as well as covered places), and loads of tattoos. Maybe this even describes you. There was a time when such accoutrements would have been taken as sure signs of mental illness. Of course, there was also a time when the spectacle of a person walking down the street while carrying on an animated conversation at high volume in the absence of any visible partner would also have been ascribed to insanity. Today, the former is written off to fashion and the latter to a cell phone call.

The line between normal or acceptable and abnormal or unacceptable is mobile. It depends in part on the local community, the times, fad and fashion, and the individual who does the observing and the judging. The guy wearing jackboots, a cut-off shirt, and a sleeveless jean jacket standing in a grocery line buying milk and cookies may or may not strike you as strange or even scary. But is he dangerous? Or is he making a fashion and lifestyle statement? You can't tell on the basis of appearance alone. If that guy does not get into your face, does not stare at you menacingly, does not gesture toward you, does not behave threateningly toward you, and does not give you a bad gut feeling, well, maybe you still don't want to strike up a conversation with him, but you have to admit that he has a right to dress as he likes and to buy all the sweet carbs and dairy products he can afford.

Look for Behavior

Chapter 1 gives you advice on "reading people," how to pick up on body language and other behavior cues that suggest someone is possibly dangerous, maybe even intentionally out to do harm. As the discussions in both of these chapters make clear, the important thing to watch for is behavior, not just static appearance.

Watch especially for how a person carries his or her arms and hands. Wild gestures or unexplainable movements may indicate trouble. Inappropriate verbal behavior—cursing under the breath or aloud, making apparently meaningless exclamations, barking, and other bizarre noises, reeling off pseudo-religious ramblings—all of these suggest a disturbed individual.

There is no best way to handle such people. In fact, you should not try to "handle" them at all. The best move is to get out of the way. Let them pass and don't confront them. Glaring eye contact may scare off a mentally stable would-be attacker—a garden-variety mugger—but it may well provoke someone who is not of sound mind, whose perception of reality is distorted. If contact is unavoidable, be direct, brief, and move on. Avoid reacting to what the person says, and don't engage in a conversation with him or her.

Hard Fact

A 2004 National Institute of Mental Health (NIMH) study revealed that about 6 percent, or 1 in 17, of Americans 18 and older suffer from a serious mental illness. Nearly half (45 percent) in this group suffer from more than one mental disorder at a given time. The 2006 NIMH Clinical Antipsychotic Trials of Intervention Effectiveness (CATIE) study suggested that about 19 percent of those suffering from serious mental illness exhibit violent behavior from time to time. The danger is greatest for those who abuse or stop taking prescribed antipsychotic medication.

Look for a Pattern

The discussion in Chapter 1 as well as above mainly concerns people you may encounter just once on campus or randomly on the street—in other words, perfect strangers. But what about your fellow students or other campus regulars, the people with whom you come into contact more or less regularly?

Although irrational outbursts of violence—on the street, in the workplace, at home, or on campus—always make the 6 o'clock news, it's actually fairly rare for someone simply to "lose it," to act out violently without any warning. As the opening of this chapter makes clear, Cho Seung Hui, the Virginia Tech shooter, exhibited a history—a pattern—of disturbing behavior before he exploded into violence. Even among the most dangerous of individuals, this is usually the case.

The following patterns of behavior are typical of a person who is, at the very least, distressed and quite possibly disturbed:

- Significant negative change in familiar behavior; for example, you've always known Mike to be a top student. Suddenly, Mike drops to the bottom of the class.

- Obvious listlessness, vacancy; looks like he or she "isn't really there."

- Repeated disruptive behavior in class or social situations

- Exaggerated "normal" emotions, such as hysterical laughter or tearfulness.

- Apparently high level of irritability.

- Unruly, abrasive, aggressive, or violent behavior.

- Obvious signs of alcohol intoxication or drug abuse.

- Strange or impaired speech.

- Garbled or disjointed expression of thoughts.

- Manifestation of extreme anxiety.

- Exaggerated inability to make decisions.

- Marked depression.

- Talk of death or suicide.

- Talk of violence or expressing a desire to commit acts of violence.

- Marked changes in personal hygiene.

- Obviously inappropriate or bizarre expression of emotion, such as laughing when someone is injured.

- Obviously inappropriate or bizarre behavior, such as talking to invisible people.

- Making any kind of threats to others.

It is the responsibility of everyone in the campus community to take note of such patterns or changes of pattern and not to ignore them in the hope that they will just go away.

Taking Action

If the pattern of behavior of someone you know changes in any of the ways just listed—or in any way that alarms you—you will need to decide on a course of action.

Talk About It

If you know the person well, you may want to express your concern and personally suggest to the person that he or she seek counseling. If you're not comfortable doing this or if you feel that you don't know the per- son well enough to do this, talk to a professor who knows the student or speak with someone at the counseling center. If you believe that the student is a danger to himself or others, speak directly with the campus police.

> **Bad Idea!**
>
> Never ignore disturbing behavior, pattern of behavior, or a disturbing change in the pattern of someone's behavior. It poses a danger to you, to the cam- pus community, and most of all to the person in question. Take action.

When you speak with someone— a professor, a counselor, or the police—do not express your opinion or judgment, but report what you have observed. Explain the basis of your concern.

Crossing the Line

In the event of an actual violent act or a threat of any kind, do not take action with the other person yourself. Report it directly to the campus police.

Nobody wants to get another person into trouble, but the following behavior clearly crosses the line and either presents an immediate danger or constitutes a warning of impending danger:

- ◆ Threats of any kind

- ◆ Graphic talk of committing violence, sex acts, or any crime

- ◆ Actual violence—striking out, punching, kicking, or fighting

- ◆ Uncontrolled or uncontrollable behavior of any kind

Even if a person makes a threat and leaves without acting on the threat, take it seriously. Call the campus police immediately. Do not ignore the outburst or dismiss it as "nothing more than stress" or a "harmless blowing off of steam." A threat is never appropriate, especially in the close community of a college campus. You may think that, by not calling the cops, you are cutting the other person a break. That is not the case. By ignoring a threat or other violent outburst—even if it is fleeting—you are endangering yourself, others, and the person who has acted out. At the very least, obviously inappropriate behavior is a cry for help. At worst, it is a prelude to catastrophe.

Look Out—for Yourself and Others

Your job is to be a student, not a cop, psychologist, judge, jury, or hall monitor. People look and act across a very broad range, and something someone does sooner or later is certain to rub you the wrong way. On such an occasion, the best response is usually just to walk away.

But when someone does or says things that alarm you, that frighten you, or that make you fear for your safety or the safety of others— including the safety of the person responsible for the behavior or the words—take action. First and foremost, do whatever you have to do to avoid putting yourself in harm's way. Then, if what you see or hear or experience seems to signal danger now or to come, call the campus police. It is your responsibility to yourself and your campus community. You may very well save more than one life.

The Least You Need to Know

- ◆ An open and tolerant attitude is no excuse for ignoring or excusing unacceptable, threatening, or violent behavior in others.

- ◆ Do not confuse deviance with diversity. Alert campus authorities to anyone who exhibits alarming or disturbing behavior or who makes threats of any kind.

- ◆ Call the campus police if you see a strange person on campus who does not seem to have legitimate business there.

- ◆ Become sensitive and alert to the warning signs of potentially violent or destructive behavior in others.

- ◆ Never ignore behavior, threats, violence, or other acts that frighten or alarm you. Do not confront disturbing or disturbed people, but do call the campus police.

Part 4

Getting Help and Helping Yourself

The concluding part of this book provides chapters on dealing effectively with health and emotional problems, including emergencies as well as more routine difficulties. Here you'll also find advice on how to get the help you need when you need it, and the bottom-line basics of self-defense on campus and off. The college campus is staffed with many professionals dedicated to helping you, but in the end, your safety and security are your responsibility. That fact is part of any college education.

13

On the Edge, Over the Edge

In This Chapter

- Emergencies and urgent situations
- Coping with stress
- Fighting fatigue
- Sadness, depression, thoughts of suicide, and anger
- Eating disorders
- Using 911 effectively

The upside of college and university life includes a new independence, the excitement of learning new things, a host of opportunities to excel, and entrance into a whole new world of acquaintances and friends. The downside may include a heavy workload, daunting intellectual challenges, pressures to perform, social pressures, deadlines, a certain amount of confusion, a fear of failure, and maybe even homesickness. College students often stay up too late, worry too much, eat too much or too little or just plain poorly, and generally stress out. There is also the college environment: a lot of people packed into a limited space means that when Jane sneezes, John catches cold.

This chapter deals with staying healthy and getting healthy, and what to do when you're feeling low.

Health Emergencies

All residential colleges and universities have a student health service. Get to know it. Know where it is, and know how to reach it. (Read more about student health services in Chapter 14.) In case of serious illness or injury, call 911 or campus security.

Emergency vs. Urgent Need

Medical emergencies are life threatening and require immediate care. They include the following:

- **Accident with injury.** Err on the side of caution. Call 911 even if the injury does not immediately seem serious.

- **Alcohol poisoning.** A person who becomes unconscious as a result of consuming alcohol (as in a binge-drinking episode) is in a potentially life-threatening situation. Call 911.

- **Anaphylaxis.** This is a severe allergic reaction, which may produce shock and life-threatening respiratory distress. Anaphylaxis may occur within minutes or even hours after exposure to an allergy-causing substance, such as insect venom (from a bite or sting), pollen, latex, certain foods, and drugs. Symptoms may include hives; marked swelling of eyes or lips; and swelling of the lining of the throat, which may cause difficulty breathing or even shock. Dizziness, mental confusion, abdominal cramping, nausea, vomiting, and diarrhea are other common symptoms of anaphylaxis. Anyone who has had anaphylaxis in the past should carry appropriate medications. Administer them. If they are unavailable, call 911 immediately.

- **Severe bleeding.** Apply pressure to control the bleeding, then call 911. Maintain pressure until help arrives.

- **Broken bones or dislocation.** These cannot always be readily diagnosed by those without medical training, but if a limb does not "look right," causes intense pain, or cannot be used, call 911.

- **Burns.** Serious burns from fire or chemicals require immediate medical aid—a call to 911.

- **Chest pain.** Always assume that this symptom is life threatening. Call 911.

- **Choking.** A choking person typically clutches at his throat. Even if he does not, look for inability to talk; difficulty breathing or noisy breathing; inability to cough forcefully; skin, lips and nails turning blue or dusky; or loss of consciousness. Perform the Heimlich maneuver, *then* call 911.

- **Drug overdose.** Call 911. Make every effort to ascertain the name of the drug and the quantity ingested.

- **Electrical shock or lightning strike.** If the person is in contact with a live wire, great care must be exercised to remove him. Touching the person while he is in contact with the electric source will cause the rescuer to be electrocuted. If the person is not breathing, begin CPR, if you have the training. Call 911.

- **Head pain.** Severe, sudden, unexplained head pain should trigger a call to 911.

- **Head trauma.** In any case of a blow to the head, call 911.

- **Heart attack.** In any case of suspected heart attack, call 911.

- **Heatstroke or sunstroke.** This is a life-threatening medical emergency. Get the person out of the sun and call 911.

- **Insect (including spider) bites and stings.** If these are accompanied by severe swelling or sickness (or other signs of anaphylaxis), call 911. If the source of the bite is known to be dangerous (a black widow or brown recluse spider, for example), call 911.

- **Poisoning.** Unless you know that the source of the poison is corrosive (strong acid or alkali), induce vomiting. Call 911. If you have immediate access to the local poison control number, call this as well.

◆ **Shock.** Shock is a common effect of blood loss, trauma, heat-stroke, allergic reactions, severe infection, poisoning, and other causes. Signs of shock include cool and clammy skin, which may appear ashen, pallid, or gray; rapid, weak pulse; slow and shallow breathing or hyperventilation (rapid or deep breathing); a drop in blood pressure; lackluster, staring eyes, sometimes with widely dilated pupils; and possible loss of consciousness, faintness, weakness, confusion, great anxiety, or excitement. If any of these signs are present—especially after injury—call 911.

◆ **Snakebite.** Any snakebite merits a call to 911. If possible, try to identify the species of snake—at least be able to describe it.

◆ **Spinal injury.** Any suspected spinal or neck injury requires that the victim *not* be moved (unless he or she is in a life-threatening situation) and an immediate call to 911.

Safe Move

Student health is on campus to help you. Usually, it is your best first resort, except in serious or life-threatening emergencies—in which case, always call 911. If student health services are temporarily unavailable, go off campus to a local primary care facility ("doc in a box") or hospital emergency room. If your own family physician is nearby, consider an appointment with him or her.

◆ **Stroke.** A stroke is caused by bleeding into the brain or interruption of normal blood flow to the brain. In either case, brain cells start dying, resulting in brain damage, permanent disability, or death. Call 911 if you or anyone else exhibits the symptoms of stroke, including any of these: sudden weakness or numbness in the face, arm, or leg—especially on one side of the body only; sudden dimness, blurring, or loss of vision, especially in one eye; loss of speech or trouble talking or understanding speech; sudden, severe headache; or unexplained dizziness.

Some other medical problems may be classed as urgent rather than emergencies. These kinds of problems require help "right away," but they are not life-threatening emergencies. You may want to call campus security or visit student health. Urgent (but non-life-threatening) situations include:

- **Animal bites.** Call campus security, which should in turn also call local animal control officers. If possible, the animal should be confined and tested for rabies. Even if rabies is ruled out, animal bites can cause severe infection. All animal bites require prompt medical attention.

- **Black eye.** Go to student health.

- **Burns.** Go to student health—unless the burn is major or extensive. For severe burns, call 911.

- **Corneal abrasion.** Any "minor" eye injury, including the persistent feeling that something is in the eye, requires a prompt examination at the student health clinic.

- **Fainting.** If you or someone you know faints, a prompt visit to student health is called for, even if there is a quick recovery.

- **Fever.** Any fever over 102°F or any fever that lasts more than a day or two warrants a trip to student health. A high fever—104°F—should be considered a medical emergency. Call 911.

- **Food-borne illness.** Symptoms of minor food poisoning include diarrhea, nausea, and vomiting. These may be treated by student health personnel, although the symptoms usually improve on their own fairly quickly. Severe food poisoning symptoms—bloody diarrhea, severe vomiting, pain, high fever, and unconsciousness—constitute a medical emergency. Call 911.

- **Foreign objects.** Any object lodged in the ear, eye, nose, or skin (such as a hard-to-remove splinter) all warrant a prompt visit to student health.

- **Gastroenteritis.** If you have a relatively minor bellyache that persists, visit student health. If you are in significant or acute pain, call 911.

- **Nosebleed.** If you cannot stop a nosebleed, go to student health.

Visit student health for any non-life-threatening complaint—or if you have a health issue you want to discuss.

Don't spend time trying to decide whether a problem is a full-blown emergency or just urgent. If a given situation prompts you to call 911, don't waste time thinking about it. Make the call right away. Let the 911 operator decide. You will not get into trouble for turning in a "false alarm."

Get Checked Out

Virtually all residential colleges and universities require new incoming students to furnish medical records, including the results of a recent examination. Typically, the examining physician—usually your family doctor—is asked to fill out a questionnaire. Proof of standard vaccinations is also required.

Hard Fact

Most state and private residential universities and colleges require students 17 years old and younger to show proof of having had a full vaccination course against diphtheria, tetanus, and pertussis (DTP) or tetanus and diphtheria (Td); polio; measles; mumps; and rubella. The requirements for older students often vary, excluding proof of polio vaccination and some of the other vaccinations as well.

You may look upon all this as just another bureaucratic hurdle you're expected to clear before the powers that be finally let you into their school—and, to some extent, you're right. However, preparing to go off to college offers *you*, not just school authorities, a golden opportunity to get a full checkup. You can address any outstanding medical issues— and that includes needed dental work!—before you go off to dorm life. With all of this out of the way, you'll have one less thing to worry about.

Vital Stats

Be sure that both you and your parents make and keep a copy of whatever records your doctor sends to your school. These contain valuable information that will help any caregiver give you the best and most appropriate care if and when you need it. At the very least, make it your responsibility to know the following about yourself:

◆ Food and medicine allergies

◆ Any medications you regularly take, including dosage

◆ Any medical conditions you have—or major medical conditions for which you have been treated in the past

◆ Any special needs you may have

◆ Complete contact information on parents or guardians, regular physician(s), and regular dentist

Stressed Out

Stress is such a common complaint among us denizens of modern civilization that we all too readily resign ourselves to it as inevitable—even normal. But think about it. Think about the word: *stress*. What happens to any physical object—a stick of wood, for example—that is continually subjected to stress?

It breaks.

Stress may be a common complaint, but it is not a normal state of being. In fact, it's no way to live. It's unpleasant, even painful in and of itself, and it may contribute to all sorts of other ailments, ranging from frequent colds and flu (because stress lowers general resistance) to long-term problems such as high blood pressure and heart disease.

College life makes a lot of demands on your time, your body, your mind, your emotions, your wallet (or that of your parents), and your ego. All of these demands tend to create stress. But that does not mean that stress is inevitable or has to be a permanent fixture of your life. You can find relief.

Safe Move

A certain amount of stress is healthy. The adrenaline you feel pumping before a big exam or a major athletic event helps you concentrate and gives you extra energy. The heightened alertness you feel, say, when you're driving in a heavy rain improves your reaction time and your general awareness. It helps you stay alive on the road. You will never lead a stress-free life. Indeed, without some stress, you probably wouldn't lead your life for long.

All Wound Up

You may know you're stressed because you simply feel that way—tense and anxious. On the other hand, you may not be aware that some of the things you are feeling some or most of the time are signs of stress. If …

- You frequently feel your heart racing no special reason

- Your palms are always sweaty

- Your hands and/or feet feel cold

- You have a lot of headaches

- Your muscles feel tight all of the time (especially neck, jaw, chest, and back muscles)

- You are often irritable, angry, tense, nervous

- You are jumpy, easily startled

- You have trouble sleeping

- You have a lot of unexplained skin breakouts

- You have appetite loss—or are *always* eating

- You have a lot of stomachaches or cramps

- You have frequent indigestion or heartburn

- You have frequent urgent diarrhea

- You sometimes can't catch your breath—you hyperventilate or breathe very shallowly

- You just don't have fun anymore

- Your nails are chewed up

- You're popping lots and lots of aspirin

- You feel anxious or scared for no particular reason

… you may be suffering from stress.

Your Best Friend Should Tell You

Another measure of your stress level is what your friends tell you. If you are repeatedly told that you look or act tense or "stressed out," or that you ought to cut back on coffee (but you don't drink coffee), pay heed. Your friends are recognizing the signs of stress, and they are giving you valuable information.

First Things First

If you have such symptoms as stomach cramps, chronic indigestion, frequent diarrhea, insomnia, headaches, muscle aches, and the like, your first move is to see a doctor. You might want to consult student health or go to your own physician. If no specific cause can be nailed down, the likely culprit is stress.

Hard Fact
Stressed out? You're not alone. A recent UCLA study reported that 30.2 percent of freshmen reported "feeling stressed" or were "frequently overwhelmed" by everything they have to do. How does this compare with the general population? Recent figures from the Centers for Disease Control (CDC) and the National Institute for Occupational Safety and Health (NIOSH) cite stress for 25 percent to 40 percent of "job burnout" cases reported by U.S. workers, and a recent Roper Starch Worldwide survey of 30,000 people between the ages of 13 and 65 in 30 countries indicated that 23 percent of women executives and professionals and 19 percent of their male peers report feeling "super-stressed."

Stress Relief

For most people, the greatest single source of stress is trying to get control of any of the hundreds of different things that make demands on us every day.

Some of these you can control, at least more or less.

For example: is the approach of a difficult midterm getting you stressed out? While you cannot control what questions your professor will ask, you can set aside time for extra study and you can round up some friends to organize a study group. You have at least some significant control over this particular stressor ("stressor" = something that causes stress).

Some things you cannot control. Learn to recognize these and to accept them. But how do you learn to tell the difference between what you can and cannot control? Try this exercise: make a list of everything that bothers you, that gets you stressed. Don't think about it. Just write. Let the words come tumbling out in a rambling laundry list. After you've spent 10 or 15 minutes writing this up, fold the paper in half and put it away overnight. On the next day, take out the list and cross out everything over which you have no control.

> **Bad Idea!**
>
> A torrent of TV, Internet, and magazine ads tout piles of over-the-counter pills and powdered supplements "guaranteed" to fight stress. Don't take any pill or supplement without consulting a medical professional. At the very least, you risk wasting your money. Far more important, you risk your health.

Now, take what's left and copy it onto a fresh sheet of paper. Number these items in order of their importance to you. Starting with number one, devise some strategies for gaining positive control of the stressor. Tackle one stressor at a time, in descending order of priority.

What should you do with the first list, the one with all the crossed-out items? Tell yourself: *I can't do anything about this stuff, so I won't worry about it.* Then rip the paper up and throw it away. You don't need it anymore. Ever.

Spill Your Guts

A lot of people find relief from stress in starting a journal. It's a kind of diary, but with a difference. Whereas a diary is a daily record of events and thoughts, a journal is more automatic and free flowing: a purging of the mind and the emotions. You are under no obligation to record events. Instead, just write about what you feel, what you fear, what worries you, what you'd like to do, and how you'd *like* to feel. Let it all come pouring out, put it away for a while, then read it over.

Keeping a journal helps you sort out your emotions and gain some perspective on them. These days, many people keep their journals on computer. There are even dedicated journal-writing programs available, such as "The Journal" (from DavidRM Software) and LifeJournal (from LifeJournal), which help stimulate, focus, and organize your thoughts.

Get a Workout

Exercise is a highly effective stress buster. Do something you enjoy: swim, play tennis, walk, run, go bowling—whatever. Work up a sweat.

Break Your Routine

People who report suffering from stress often say that they are "in a rut." Get out of the rut by doing something different. Take a break. Go off campus. Get away from your familiar world, if only for a few hours at a time.

Call a Friend—or a Few Friends

Do something with others. Go out to lunch, go to a movie—anything to get you out and about and among people.

Shun Stress Amplifiers

Various things we consume, including junk food, sugary foods and drinks, caffeinated beverages, energy drinks, alcohol, and cigarettes, amplify stress. There is a paradox here, because, in the short run, they may relieve stress, serving as a kind of pick-me-up, but sooner rather than later, there's a letdown, which usually comes with a crash. When you're feeling stressed, avoid substances that amplify the bad feelings.

Worn Out

People of college age are supposed to enjoy the unlimited energy reserves of youth. They never get tired. Ever.

Right?

Of course not. College is a busy time, with lots of hard work, plenty of stressful situations, and multiple demands on your time. Sleep is often a rare commodity, and if you live in a bustling dorm, it may be, at times, nearly impossible to come by.

If you feel worn out and tired much of the time, look for a cause or causes. The most obvious question is always: Are you getting enough sleep? A little less obvious is this follow-up: Are you getting a good, satisfying, refreshing sleep?

If the answer to either of these is no, find a way to get the sleep—and the quality of sleep—you need. This may include going to bed earlier, asking roommates to come and go more quietly, and avoiding stressful activities at bedtime, such as cramming for an exam or trying to balance your checkbook.

Little Black Book

A lot of people have trouble sleeping. Browse the following websites for information on sleep disorders and how to cope with them:

www.sleepdisorderchannel.net/osa

www.aafp.org/afp/991115ap/2279.html

www.stanford.edu/~dement/apnea.html

www.healthysleeping.com/sleep/cause.asp

www.personalhealthzone.com/insomniacauses.html

http://sleepdisorders.about.com/cs/dsps/a/nightowl_2.htm

Other common causes of fatigue include overwork, overpartying, consumption of alcohol (in any amount), consumption of caffeine and energy drinks (in any amount), overworry, and lack of physical exercise. These are factors you can eliminate or alter. Give it a try, but if you still feel tired no matter what you do, even if you get a good night's sleep, and if you can think of no reason why you should feel tired, pay a visit to student health or to your own doctor.

Sad and Lonely

Watch a few minutes of television commercials, and the message is clear: everyone should be happy all of the time. All you need are the right clothes, the right credit card, the right car, the right breakfast cereal, the right deodorant ….

We live in a society that portrays sadness as a disease—but one that's easily cured by the right merchandise. The fact is, however, that sadness is an emotion, a normal response to certain events, experiences, words, sights, or thoughts. There is no way to avoid occasional sadness. Indeed, if you were always able to avoid it—if you never felt sad—*that* would be strange and, well, sad.

College life has many joys, but it also has its share of reasons for grief. You may miss home, including family, friends, and pets; you may be in the middle of a difficult time with a boyfriend or girlfriend; you may experience a loss; you may simply feel that you don't fit in.

If you can pin down a cause for your feelings of sadness, you can try to change how you feel by doing something about the cause. Sadness, however, is more difficult to cope with when you can't pin down a cause, when the feeling is just there.

What to Do About the Blues

Many of the steps you might try to relieve stress may also lift your spirits if you are feeling sad. Additionally, an obvious, commonsense antidote to sadness is laughter. Try any or all of the following:

- Treat yourself to a television sitcom or two. These are best watched with a friend.

- Rent or go to a funny movie—as a rule, the sillier the better.

- Get to a newsstand and buy a humor magazine.

- Buy a joke book.

- Spend 15 minutes a day on the Internet searching for jokes based on bodily functions, especially those having to do with digestion and elimination.

When Nothing Works

If you find that nothing lifts your spirits, and especially if you always feel low, regardless of what's going on around you, you may have clinical depression, a disorder that's often physically based and that certainly can be effectively treated by a physician. If any of the following feelings describe you, visit student health or your family doctor:

- Persistently sad or both sad and anxious

- Persistently feeling "empty"

- Feeling hopeless or pessimistic most of the time

- Feeling guilty or worthless

- Always feeling helpless

- Loss of interest or pleasure in things that you used to enjoy

- Feeling drained most of the time

- Difficulty focusing and concentrating

- Persistent difficulty making decisions

- Insomnia, including waking up very early

- Oversleeping—a desire to stay in bed

- Appetite loss

- Habitual overeating

- Unexplained irritability and/or restlessness

- Physical symptoms for which no physical cause can be found, especially headaches and digestive disorders

- Suicidal thoughts

> **Little Black Book**
>
> The U.S. Department of Health and Human Services maintains the National Suicide Prevention Lifeline, which serves more than 45,000 callers monthly. Call 1-800-273-TALK (8255).

If you find yourself thinking about death or suicide, get help. Call the campus counseling service. If you feel that you are up against the wall—especially if you think you might purposely hurt yourself—call 911.

Mad as Hell

From childhood on, most of us are taught that anger is a "bad" thing. Of course, this doesn't prevent us from getting angry from time to time, but it often has the effect of prompting us to deny or suppress our anger. Emotions, pleasant or unpleasant, require more energy to suppress than to express. If you deny or suppress whatever it is you're feeling, chances are you're going to be stressed out and feeling tired— a lot.

Everyone gets angry. The most effective way to deal with anger is to identify the cause of the feeling and try to do something about it. Does your roommate keep late hours, make too much noise, and wake you up? If so, does this make you mad? Then talk to your roommate. Explain what effect her actions are having on your sleep. Ask her to try to keep more reasonable hours or to make an extra effort to come in quietly. Do something about the source of the emotion.

If you find that you are often angry without a reason you can identify, you are probably suffering from stress. Take any or all of the steps listed earlier to reduce the stress in your life. If nothing seems to help, contact the campus counseling service. Walking around angry is not healthy—for you or those around you.

Eating Disorders

In recent years, physicians and psychologists have been paying increasing attention to eating disorders, the most prominent of which are anorexia and bulimia (also called anorexia nervosa and bulimia nervosa).

Anorexia is extreme loss of appetite or reduction of food intake, typically to dangerously low levels of a few hundred calories per day—low enough to cause malnutrition and even symptoms of starvation, including life-threatening weight loss.

Bulimia causes a person to eat very large amounts of food in a very short period. This "binging" is often followed by "purging"—self-induced vomiting or the use of excessive amounts of laxative products. (People who binge without purging are often diagnosed as having "binge eating disorder" rather than bulimia.)

The dangers of eating disorders include poor nutrition and malnutrition—which can make one vulnerable to many diseases and disorders—and even starvation, ending in death. Self-induced vomiting can cause harmful chemical imbalances in the body, injury to the lining of the esophagus and throat, and irreversible damage to tooth enamel. Untreated, eating disorders can bring depression, anxiety, and general misery. In extreme cases, these disorders are life threatening.

If you're concerned that you have an eating disorder, consult the medical providers at student health or visit your family physician. Some physical signs of eating disorders include …

> **Hard Fact**
>
> According to the U.S. National Institute of Mental Health, between 5 and 10 percent of girls and women (5 to 10 million people) and 1 million boys and men suffer from eating disorders, including anorexia, bulimia, and binge eating disorder.

- Significant weight loss or gain.
- Frequent fatigue.
- Often feeling cold (when others do not).
- Sore throat (from frequent vomiting).
- Loss of tooth enamel (from frequent vomiting).
- General appearance of illness—pale complexion, dull hair, hair loss.

Besides eating too much or too little (or not eating at all), self-induced vomiting, and the use of laxatives and diet pills, other symptoms of eating disorders include dissatisfaction with how you look (always too fat or too thin); self-imposed isolation from others; becoming an exercise fanatic (never feeling that you can work out enough or burn enough calories); and obsessing about food or weight.

The 411 on 911

The emotional and physical problems college students sometimes encounter in themselves, their roommates, and their friends have two things in common: they can all be treated—if not cured, at least made better; and they are all harmful or dangerous *if they are ignored*. The bottom line: get help, and urge your friends to get help.

If you feel you or someone else has a problem that cannot wait, an emergency, call 911. Don't worry about calling in a "false alarm." If the sickness, injury, behavior, or complaint makes you even consider calling 911, dial now. You won't get into trouble, and no one will holler at you or laugh at you for doing it.

We've all seen hundreds of TV shows in which someone calls 911, but when you actually have to make the call, you may feel scared and confused. Here's all you need to do:

- The 911 operator needs to know who you are, exactly where you are, and why you are calling (the nature of the emergency). Identify yourself. Say where you are. Explain what has happened and what is happening.

- Take a deep breath and try to remain calm. Speak as slowly and as distinctly as you can.

- Answer all of the operator's questions as fully and as accurately as possible. These will probably include *What is the emergency? Where are you? Who is with you?*

- Do *not* hang up until the 911 operator tells you to do so.

In an emergency, waste no time trying to decide who to call—campus security, student health, campus counseling, or 911. The 911 operator is trained to take your information and to make a rapid evaluation of what help to send right away, including the campus police, the city police, or an ambulance. Just make the call.

The Least You Need to Know

- An emergency is a life-threatening situation, whereas an urgent situation requires prompt attention, but is not life threatening. When in doubt, always call 911.

- Stress, fatigue, and sadness are common complaints. You can take steps to help yourself and to get help from others.

- If you are frequently or always sad or have thoughts of death and suicide, contact student health, the campus counseling service, or your own doctor right away. In an emergency, call 911 or the National Suicide Prevention Lifeline at 1-800-273-TALK (8255).

- If you have little or no appetite, eat very little, routinely eat too much, binge on food, or binge and purge, go to student health or consult your family doctor.

- Call 911 in any situation that seems to you to be an emergency. The 911 operator is trained to determine and dispatch the appropriate help.

Chapter 14

The Campus Helpers

In This Chapter

- Help's there when you need it
- Advice with academic issues
- About financial aid
- The student health center
- Psychological counseling and spiritual guidance
- On-campus cops

Your high school guidance counselor hammered it into your head: college demands a lot more responsibility from you than high school ever did. Ready or not, college is more about being an adult than it is about being a student. You are expected to take charge of yourself and to look after yourself.

Up to a point.

With apologies to the nation's high school guidance counselors, the reality of college is that the typical campus community offers a sturdier and more extensive social safety net than you are likely to find anywhere else in American life. You may be on your own, but you are hardly left alone. When you need help—and everybody needs help sometimes—you won't have to look far.

A Band of Brothers—and Sisters

The average college or university campus offers an array of professionals to help out with academic and financial matters, to look out for your health, to provide psychological counseling, and to protect your life and your property. Most campuses also offer connections to people who can address your religious or spiritual needs, if you have any.

The campus is a community. As with any community, the professional helpers are important; but no community can exist by relying exclusively on professionals. A community succeeds in proportion to the respect, concern, and care its members show for one another.

Compete—but Care

College can be a very competitive place. There's nothing wrong with that, as long as you also realize that you are in it—in this experience and in this place—together. Adopt a helping attitude toward your friends and fellow students. Be there for them. Let them talk things out with you. Cultivate a band of brothers and sisters in whom you can confide. When you are trying to make a decision about what class to take, what professor is best for you, what cell phone provider to sign up with, or what's edible in the cafeteria, ask around. Seek and share experiences and opinions.

Safe Move _____

Not every conversation has to be an intimate heart-to-heart or a profound philosophical discourse. Small talk—about a favorite TV show, an intriguing blog, a new pair of shoes, even the weather—is the glue that cements most relationships you'll have on campus. Talk to people, especially about what interests them. Listen and respond. Soon you'll find yourself with a band of brothers and sisters.

One Step Beyond

A community needs more than professional helpers, but it *does* need those helpers. Make friends, talk to your friends, ask for opinions and advice, but know when to step beyond your friends to get professional advice and help.

If you have an issue relating to your physical or emotional health, if you have a legal question, or if you have a financial problem, go to the paid professional experts your campus employs and makes available to you. Don't put your friends in the position of advising you on matters of life and death or your legal and financial well-being. Everyone is entitled to an opinion, but the fact is that some opinions are better informed (and therefore more useful) than others. Moreover, when you've had a nagging headache for the past week, you don't want your roommate's opinion on what's wrong, you want the medical professionals at student health to find out what's wrong and fix it or send you to somebody who can.

Who Ya Gonna Call?

How do you find the campus helper most appropriate to your needs? You have at least three resources:

- ◆ Almost all colleges and universities publish a student handbook, which includes a directory of campus services, complete with phone numbers.

- ◆ These days it is the rare institution that does not have an elaborate website, which includes an interactive directory of campus services. Many of these services maintain their own websites, linked to the main college or university site, so that they are no more than a mouse click away. Just about every department or campus service provider has an e-mail address in addition to a phone number.

- ◆ Campus services are typically described in the annual catalog of courses your institution publishes. Many colleges and universities publish these in print as well as online.

Safe Move

In an emergency—any situation in which the life and safety of you or someone else is in jeopardy—don't spend time looking up or figuring out who to call. Dial 911 or your campus police department. The operator who answers is trained to connect you with the help appropriate to the situation.

Academic Assistance and Advice

At the heart of the college experience is academics. Whatever else a college or university is, it is, after all, a school. But what does academic assistance and advice have to do with campus safety? Just this: to the extent that your academic career is successful and satisfying, you are more likely to be happy, healthy, and secure in college. Conversely, to the extent that your academic career disappoints you and causes you anxiety, you are likely to suffer emotionally and physically, and these problems can have a nasty, negative, even destructive impact on the decisions you make regarding behavior of all kinds.

Your Advisor

Most undergraduate colleges and universities assign each incoming freshman an academic advisor during the summer before the fall semester. Advisors are sometimes professors and sometimes members of the academic advising staff—that is, full-time advisors. In either case, the advisor's job is—guess what?—to advise you on all academic matters.

Ask for advice not only on classes that will satisfy core requirements but that also help you to explore the major or majors that most interest you. You should also feel free to ask what courses most new incoming students typically take and when they typically take them. Finally, don't neglect the nitty-gritty about the class registration process, important deadlines, and procedures for changing your schedule, including dropping or adding classes.

Rely on your advisor—up to a point. Some advisors are self-starters. They will volunteer just about all the information you could possibly need or want. But many advisors need to be activated by your questions.

Generally speaking, to get good advice—about anything, anywhere, anytime—ask good questions. When you talk to your advisor, come prepared with the questions you want answered.

Seek a Balance

One key goal you should share with your advisor is that of achieving balance. Early on, balance required courses (core courses) with courses that relate to your primary interests (the major or majors you are considering) and with elective courses that may open up new areas of interest or that present a special challenge or creative opportunity. Seek advice on the appropriate course load.

You were admitted to the college or university you now attend because administrators and faculty, after reviewing your high school transcript, your application, your test scores, and whatever else you submitted when you applied, believe that you will succeed. No college admits a student it believes will fail. No college tries to flunk a student out. Your advisor is there to help both you and the college realize a mutual expectation of success. Approach the advisor with a positive attitude. That is the way he or she approaches you.

Financial Aid

For a great many students, the one thing that creates more anxiety than academic demands and academic performance is money—or the lack thereof. Be assured that the people who run your school share your anxiety. They're worried about money, too.

Long gone are the days when academia considered itself an ivory tower kingdom far above the peasantry who deal in dollars and cents. Shortly after you receive your letter of acceptance to the school of your choice, that school's financial aid office will contact you.

Yes, the financial aid office is concerned about your needs. But its concern is firmly based on the understanding that, by finding ways to satisfy your financial needs, the school will find a way to keep paying for the buildings, professors, equipment, and everything else that goes into providing you with an education. You and your school are in this together. You *both* need financial aid.

Pay Attention, Read the Fine Print, Respond

Throughout the summer before you start your first semester—and periodically throughout your college career—the financial aid office will communicate with you through the mail and perhaps by e-mail. Carefully read everything you receive. Start a financial aid folder and throw nothing away. Respond to all questions and fill out all forms in a timely manner, well before stated deadlines. If you have any questions, don't guess at the answers. Call the financial aid office and ask.

Hard Fact
According to a recent College Board survey, about 70 percent of students attending four-year schools pay less than $8,000 for tuition and fees, thanks to some $122 billion in aid disbursed each year.

The staff of the financial aid office is not a bunch of bureaucrats hired to put obstacles in your way. Their job is to help you. If you are more comfortable with the most cynical view, they are there to help you because, by getting you the money you need, they ensure the college gets the money *it* needs. But no matter how you view the job of the financial aid office staff, they are your best expert source of information on aid programs the school offers, federal financial aid programs, scholarships and grants from all sorts of donors, and federal and state rules and regulations governing financial aid. Make extensive use of this expert resource. Whenever possible, speak to the same person in the financial aid office who has helped you in the past. Continuity and familiarity with your circumstances are both helpful to getting aid matters settled quickly and advantageously.

Keep Track

Keep copies of every single piece of paper (or electronic communication) you receive from or send to the financial aid office or to any other scholarship, aid, or grant office. Take notes during any conversations you have with the financial aid office. File everything in your financial aid folder for safekeeping, and make sure you have ready access to the material when you need it.

Let Your Parents in on It All

Just when everyone's been telling you that you're on your own now, the matter of financial aid requires you to work more closely than ever with your parents. Many of the questions on financial aid forms relate to your family's income, and the Free Application for Federal Student Aid (FAFSA) form that every student who applies for any kind of financial aid must fill out requires information from your parents' federal tax returns. You will probably also have to supply the financial aid office with an actual copy of your tax return as well as the returns of your parents shortly after the income tax due date of April 15.

Keep your folks up to speed. Help them with the paperwork necessary to help you.

About Loans

The great thing about scholarships and grants is that you don't have to pay them back. The downside is that not everyone qualifies for them, and even for those who do qualify, scholarship and grant money rarely covers all the expenses of a college education. To a greater or lesser degree, educational loans figure into almost every student's financial aid picture.

Your financial aid office will guide you through the application process for such low-interest federal loans as Stafford Loans and Perkins Loans. You may have to be interviewed by the financial aid office, either in person or in a group; many schools offer an online process.

Don't make the mistake of assuming that loans are only for students whose families fall below a certain income level. While it's true that the student must demonstrate financial need to qualify for a fully sub-sidized federal loan, nonsubsidized loans are available to everyone, regardless of financial need. The downside of these? Nonsubsidized loans cost more.

A loan is a loan. That means you have to pay it back. Government-subsidized loans pay the interest for you while you are in college. With nonsubsidized loans, interest accrues, even while you are in college. You may have to pay interest during your college years or the interest may be partially or wholly deferred until sometime after graduation. Either way, you pay.

Hard Fact
Some loans are made to you, the student. These may be supplemented with loans made to your parents, either through private home equity loan programs or through the federal PLUS program, which provides relatively low-interest loans to parents for the purposes of helping to finance their children's education. Your financial aid office can supply information and application forms for federal PLUS loans.

Buyer Beware

A nonsubsidized loan is a commercial loan—a product. Just because you are using the money for school or because your financial aid office has recommended a particular bank or loan company, there's no guarantee that you are getting the best available interest rate and terms. Work with your parents to find the best loan you can get. Ask the following questions (and be sure you get answers you understand):

- What are the loan's terms?
- How much will I owe when I graduate?
- What are the minimum monthly payments?
- What is the interest rate (APR)?
- Is the interest rate fixed or variable? (If variable, how will it be adjusted and when? Is there an interest cap?)
- Does the loan require any upfront fees?

The Goal of Financial Aid

Obviously, your goal should be to work with the financial aid office and—quite possibly—outside lenders to put together a package that will finance your education. More than that, however, you should aim for a package that provides the money you need as well as a level of emotional comfort and security.

Student Health Services

Every major university and even most small colleges have a student health office or student health center. In some universities that include a medical school and are associated with a teaching hospital, student health is a full-scale primary care center and emergency room open 24 hours a day, 7 days a week. In other places, student health may be a primary care center that is open a certain number of hours per day and may be closed or staffed on a reduced basis during the weekend.

Generally speaking, you should regard the student health center as an ambulatory health care clinic—that is, a place to go to if you are well enough to walk in. In a health emergency, call 911, and if you have an urgent—but nonemergency—health problem after student health hours, get yourself to the hospital emergency room.

 Safe Move

Some student health offices invite walk-ins, but, increasingly, they require an appointment—just as your family doctor does. If your student health service offers visits by appointment, always make an appointment.

Student health is the place to seek treatment for minor injuries and for routine illnesses. It's also a great source of information and counseling on all questions you have relating to your health. If your issue cannot be fully addressed at the student health facility, the doctor or nurse practitioner or other medical professional you consult there will direct you to the best place to find help.

Wellness

These days, medical practitioners put increasing emphasis on staying well, which they believe is a far more effective approach to maintaining your health than seeking a cure after you are already sick. If your school's student health service has a wellness center, be sure to check it out. You will find it a valuable resource for advice on healthy living, including health and nutrition assessments, wellness seminars, and other consultations.

Cost

Most student health services are financed by student health fees that are assessed as part of your tuition; therefore, most services are provided at no extra per-visit cost. Some treatments, such as flu shots, may require a fee, but almost certainly, the fee will be lower than what your family physician charges.

Special Health Needs

Virtually all colleges and universities require you to fill out a medical entrance form when you enroll. The form will probably include space for you to list and describe any special health needs you have. Often, you will be asked to furnish an explanatory letter from your health-care provider. It is your responsibility to notify the university or college— usually through the student health center—of any special needs you have. Like all other medical information you share with school health providers, this information will be kept in strictest confidence.

Do I Still Need Insurance?

If your college or university is giving you "free" routine medical care, you might wonder if you or your parents still need to pay for additional medical insurance.

The simple answer is yes.

> **Hard Fact**
>
> Keeping your medical records confidential is not just a matter of ethical policy for your school, it is an issue of law. The Health Insurance Portability and Accountability Act of 1996 protects people from having their medical histories accessed or made public without their permission.

Most likely, student health services will be available to you only when you are enrolled as a student, which may exclude the period between semesters and certainly excludes summer vacation—unless you are enrolled in classes during a summer semester. More important, treatment of major illnesses, surgeries, consultations with specialists, and many diagnostic procedures are simply unavailable from student health.

Chances are, you are covered by your parents' health insurance policy—though they will need to make sure that their insurance carrier knows that you are a full-time student, since most family coverage ends for a dependent at age 18, unless he or she is a full-time student. If you are not covered, you should consider purchasing supplementary insurance to cover major medical contingencies.

Psychological Counseling

Most colleges and universities make psychological counseling available to students. In some schools, counselors work out of the student health center; other schools maintain a separate counseling center. Typically, the counseling staff consists of professional counselors and psychologists, who (in bigger universities) may be assisted by graduate students studying clinical psychology.

Counseling centers usually offer confidential assistance with academic, career, and personal concerns. In addition to one-on-one counseling, some centers include a library of resource materials to assist with career and other life choices and even such resources as interactive computer programs to help you make important decisions. The counseling center may also offer a psychological and cognitive testing service to help you investigate your occupational interests and personality traits.

> **Safe Move**
>
> In the event of a psychological emergency—drug overdose, erratic or dangerous behavior, suicidal talk, thoughts, threats, or attempt—call 911.

The counseling center is a good resource to help you manage an emotional crisis, but it's also a place to explore more general issues of personal growth and development.

Spiritual Resources

Many private, non-state-supported schools are associated with particular churches or religions and have on-campus chapels and a college chaplain or chaplains. Such schools typically offer spiritual counseling for their students.

State colleges and universities are governed by the constitutionally mandated separation of church and state. Consequently, these institutions usually do not offer institutionalized counseling by clergy.

Both private and public colleges and universities do typically host a number of religiously oriented student organizations, which are not funded by the school. If religion is an important part of your life, consider joining one of these groups, which can connect you with a local church, synagogue, mosque, or temple.

Campus Cops

The campus police department or security office is the police authority for the college community. In an emergency, you can always dial 911, but it's also a very good idea to know the direct emergency number for your campus police. Add it to your cell phone speed dial.

Campus policing ranges from unarmed security patrols to full-scale, armed, professional police officers. If you dial 911 in response to a campus emergency, most likely the campus cops will be the first responders.

A patrol unit or patrol division is the most highly visible component of any police department. Officers in cars—and also, perhaps, on foot, on bike, and on motorcycle—patrol the campus and (often) adjacent areas 24 hours a day, 7 days a week. They are the beat cops of the college campus. The police departments of larger universities usually include more than one unit or division.

A crime prevention unit prepares and distributes to the college community crime prevention and awareness information and may develop and conduct a variety of crime awareness programs. This unit may also have the primary responsibility for compiling and analyzing campus crime data in accordance with the Clery Act (see Chapter 2).

Larger departments may include a separate criminal investigations division, responsible for the investigation of crimes against persons and property. Depending on the nature of the crime, this division often works in close cooperation with city, county, or state police departments.

In addition to protection and crime-related functions, campus police usually are responsible for maintaining the school's lost and found department and administering various security systems, including electronic card access systems. Traffic and parking management are also typical police functions—as are collecting parking fines.

If you are a victim of a crime on campus, make a full report to the campus police. Depending on the nature and circumstances of the crime you are reporting, the campus police will advise you on whether you should make a separate report directly to other police authorities as well. If your property is stolen or lost, file a full report with the campus police—*after* you visit the lost and found.

Campus police and security officers are there to serve and protect you and the rest of the campus community. They deserve the same respect and cooperation that you give to city, county, or state officers. On most larger campuses, the police are sworn peace officers, who have met municipal or state training and qualification standards and who have authority and responsibility comparable or equal to that of police officers in any other department. On some campuses, they are even more highly trained than police officers in the surrounding community.

The Least You Need to Know

♦ College life is about taking responsibility for yourself, but that doesn't mean you have to go it alone. Building a truly supportive community starts with you and your fellow students.

♦ Take advantage of the array of professional help your campus offers: academic counselors, financial aid personnel, medical professionals, psychological counselors, and the campus police.

♦ Investigate the helping resources available on your campus. Your school's website, student handbook, and annual catalog should have the information you need.

♦ In any emergency in which safety, health, or life are immediately threatened, call 911.

Chapter **15**

Defending Your Life

In This Chapter

- ◆ Avoiding danger by listening to your gut
- ◆ Living safely off campus
- ◆ Cell phone smarts
- ◆ How to "read" risky places and dangerous people
- ◆ What to do if you're attacked
- ◆ Self-defense techniques

Human beings are equipped by nature with certain survival mechanisms, but we are also propelled through our lives by the unshakeable conviction that, as far as really bad things go, "it won't happen to me." Strange as it may seem, this built-in denial mechanism is part of our human survival apparatus, too. After all, a life lived in perpetual dread of attack would be no life at all. Nevertheless, it can be fatal to allow denial to take over completely.

Bad things happen. They happen to people. We're all people. So they can happen to any of us. On campus or off, therefore, we all have a responsibility to defend our lives.

Gut Checks

Denial is a powerful impulse. Too many of us learn in life to deny a lot of things—financial problems, relationship problems, substance abuse problems, the list goes on and on. The most destructive kind of denial, however, is denial of our own feelings, our own gut instincts.

Nature prepares each of us to survive. If you touch a hot pan, you pull your fingers away from it—automatically—and you probably wouldn't even think of denying the impulse to pull back. Similarly, our senses pick up on danger signals in the environment, signals we might not even be consciously aware of. Dark, isolated corners of the campus. A figure following too closely behind us, turning when we turn. Disturbing eye-to-eye contact with a total stranger. None of these are overt threats, and yet all send a shiver down the spine and send a message to the brain: *Something isn't right here. Get out. Get away.*

When your gut talks to you, listen.

> **Bad Idea!**
>
> In college, everyone says you're supposed to be grown up and act like an adult. Okay. That's a reasonable goal. But don't interpret your fears as "childish." If a situation, an environment, or a person frightens you, there's probably a good reason for the feeling. Don't ignore it. Prepare to get out, get away, and, if necessary, defend your life.

Get Out, Get Away

If you find yourself somewhere that gives you a gut feeling of danger, don't ignore, dismiss, or suppress the feeling. Get out and get away.

Identify a safe place and go to it. Readily available safe places include large stores or supermarkets, public libraries, banks, office buildings, restaurants—any place with people and a telephone. If it's late at night, a convenience store or an all-night pharmacy or even a well-lit service station are good options. In residential areas, go to a well-maintained, well-lit house. Knock on the door, identify yourself, and explain the problem.

On your way to a safe place, get your cell phone out. If you feel immi-
nently menaced, call 911, but keep walking. Even if you don't feel that
danger is certain, pretend to talk. As you do, make the conversation
look purposeful, and keep scanning your environment. Show whoever
is out there that you are fully alert and that you are not really alone, but
are in contact with others.

Listen to your gut, but don't let your gut feelings overwhelm you. Keep
your eyes and ears open to what is actually around you.

Don't stare straight ahead or look downward. Be alert and aware, and
show the world that you are alert and aware. Scan your environment,
moving your head from left to right. Keep your eyes moving. Glance
rather than stare. Do not become fixated on any one object.

If you see a potential threat, do not look away. Glance and then glare at
the person to let him know that you are aware of his presence and that
you are prepared for anything he may do. It is best not to make direct
eye contact, but glare *through* the other person by looking just over his
shoulder. Keep the angle of your vision high. The message you are conveying is that he has lost the element of surprise. You're ready for him.
In the meantime, keep heading for a safe place.

Just as you should not let your feelings blind you to the environment,
don't let them make you deaf, either. When you feel scared, you naturally start breathing faster and your heart begins to pound. As fear
increases, you begin to hear the sound of your own breathing, the
sound of your heart pounding, and the pulsing rush of blood. Soon,
these become just about the only things you hear.

All of this is a natural physiological response to fear. The danger is that
these sensations may turn you inward, getting you so self-involved that
you lose touch with your surroundings.

Don't try to ignore or deny your fear. Don't dismiss your feelings
as childish. But do start consciously taking deep, measured breaths.
Controlling your anxious breathing will help you stay tuned to sounds
from outside. Concentrate on listening. As you continually scan the
environment visually, scan it with your ears as well. And keep moving
toward a place of safety.

Assess Your Surroundings

Instinct is important, but one of the really good things about being a human being is that you don't have to depend on instinct alone. Use your intellect and common sense to assess the security of a given environment.

Look around your campus and the neighborhood surrounding your school. Study these environments with your personal security in mind. What are the safest routes to get you to the places you usually go? Where are the campus emergency phones located? Where are the safe places?

Look at your environment after dark—the campus, the classroom buildings, the residence halls, and so on. What buildings are well lit? What pathways are open and adequately lit? What security features do you see? Are parking lots fenced? Are residence hall doors locked or usually propped open? Where is the campus security office/police station? Is there evidence of police patrol? Are campus shuttle buses available on a frequent schedule? How late does the shuttle service run? Are after-dark escorts available? If so, be sure to program the appropriate campus phone number into your cell phone.

Don't forget to check out fraternity row on campus and the local clubs adjacent to campus. If possible, drive through these areas on weekend nights. Is it a wild scene or are people behaving responsibly? Is there evidence of widespread binge drinking? Does the situation look to be on the verge of perpetual riot? Or is it controlled?

Survey your environment and think. Identify the safe places and the risky places. Know when to avoid the latter.

Living Off Campus: Special Considerations

Throughout most of this book, we've assumed that you are either living on campus in a residence hall or commuting. If you live in an off-campus apartment or other housing, you'll need to take on even more responsibility to ensure your safety.

Roommates and Neighbors

Get to know those who live with you. That includes roommates and neighbors. Create with them a miniature community. Look out for each other. Make sure you have your roommate's cell phone number and other relevant contact information, including his or her family's phone number. Create a bond with a neighbor or two. Give them your home number as well as your cell phone number.

Make certain that your family knows where you are and how to reach you. Give them all of your address information, e-mail address, and all telephone numbers. It's a very good idea to give your family your roommate's contact information as well. Certainly, they should have all relevant college administration numbers.

Guard Your Castle

Realtors always say that the three most important considerations in real estate are *location*, *location*, and *location*. In the case of off-campus housing, however, these criteria are generally edged out by *cost*, *cost*, and *cost*, always modified by the adjectives *cheap*, *cheap*, and *cheap*.

Your college or university may maintain a list of approved off-campus housing, places that meet certain minimum standards of safety, livability, and affordability. But it's up to you to do a full evaluation. The unfortunate fact of life is that "cheap" can mean "less than safe" or even downright "dangerous."

Little Black Book
Your best resource for identifying off-campus housing that meets minimum safety requirements is the housing office of your college or university. Many schools maintain websites with guides to off-campus housing, including a list of safety requirements.

Guard Against Fire

The greatest hazard we face in our homes is fire. Every city and town has building codes and fire regulations, but there's no guarantee that all off-campus student housing meets every requirement. Here are some guidelines to help ensure your safety:

◆ Make certain your apartment has smoke alarms and that they are in working order. If alarms are not installed, install them. Check them monthly. Replace batteries as needed.

◆ Have at least two working flashlights available in the apartment. Check and replace batteries regularly.

◆ If the apartment is equipped with fire extinguishers, check their gauges and inspection tags. If there are no extinguishers, purchase one at a hardware or home store. Many inexpensive extinguishers are available.

◆ Don't get careless with cooking, and unplug all heating appliances (space heaters, toasters, toaster ovens, coffeemakers) when you are not using them. Never leave these on and unattended.

◆ Never smoke in bed.

◆ Don't leave burning candles, incense, or other open flames unattended.

◆ Never overload electrical circuits by plugging multiple appliances into a single outlet.

◆ Inspect the electrical power cords of all appliances, including televisions, lamps, and computers. Any frayed or damaged insulation can easily result in fire.

◆ Make certain that you can access all doors and that they all work. For security, an external door may automatically lock when it is closed, but you should be able to open it from the inside at any time without a key. Basement doors are often blocked by stored items and junk. Make sure they are clear.

◆ Agree with your roommate on an evacuation plan.

Bad Idea!

In most college towns, property owners are willing to rent out just about *any* space as student housing, and they often sneak under the radar of building codes to do so. Be especially careful about basement apartments. Any bedroom located in a basement must have an exit other than the stairway. This means a standard door to the outside of the building, not just a window. Don't rent a basement space that does not have a direct exit to the outside. In a fire, this could be a matter of life or death.

Guard Against Burglars

After fireproofing your digs, do some burglarproofing. This does not take a lot of money or sophistication. Remember, most burglars are opportunists. They are not professionals in search of a challenge, burning with an ambition to break into Fort Knox. They're looking for a pushover. Make your place hard to break into, and most burglars will move on. Keep these tips in mind:

♦ The vast majority of burglars come through the front door. Make your front door as secure as possible. With an exterior door, the more solid, the better. Hollow-core doors can be kicked in easily.

♦ Check the doorframe. Be certain that it's sturdy and in good repair. If the frame is splintered or fragile, a kick will not just break down the door, it will easily carry the frame with it.

♦ Exterior doors should be secured with high-quality deadbolt locks. Lock your door when you leave, of course, but also keep it locked when you are at home.

♦ An apartment door should be equipped with a peephole that is clean and unscratched, so that you can clearly see who's at your door before you open it.

♦ Windows should be securely lockable from the inside.

♦ Ideally, you should avoid first-floor, street-level apartments. If possible, opt for a second floor or higher.

You may have only limited control over what is immediately outside of your apartment building, but look for the following:

♦ **Absence of clutter.** It's especially important that tools and ladders *not* be left outside, where a burglar can use them to break in.

♦ **Maximum visibility.** Trees and shrubs may make a building more attractive, but they can also serve as hiding places for people who mean you harm.

♦ **Lighting.** All entrances should be well lit. Lights activated by motion detectors are a very good idea.

If necessary, talk to your landlord about providing or improving these safety conditions.

Behave Yourself

In addition to physical safeguards you can install in your apartment, you can adopt certain patterns of personal behavior that will make your home more secure.

To begin with, don't show off your wealth. For most students, this is hardly a problem—but if you happen to have fancy clothes, a costly car, an elaborate home entertainment system, or the like, you are making yourself an attractive target. The more effectively that you can create the impression that you have little or nothing of value, the less interest a potential burglar will show in your home.

Vary your routine and don't announce your absence. Even casual burglars devote time to casing potential targets. They observe when occupants leave and when they come home. The more regular your routine, the more attractive your home as a target for break-in. Burglars don't like to be surprised.

> **Safe Move**
>
> Make your answering machine or voice mail message as neutral as possible. Do not provide a name, and do not announce that you are not at home. Instead, simply say, "You have reached 555-555-5555. Please leave a message."

Burglars have ears as well as eyes. If you're going to be away from home for a while—on vacation, say—don't announce it to the world. Certainly, you will want to inform a few trusted friends, your family, and a *trusted* neighbor, but don't talk about your plans freely to anyone who does not need to know.

Take steps to make your place look occupied—even when it isn't:

◆ Put some of your interior lights on outlet timers. The kind that can be programmed to turn on and off at variable times are best.

◆ Ask a *trusted* neighbor or friend to pick up your mail. If you are going to be away for a while, go to the post office and fill out an order to hold your mail.

◆ If you subscribe to any home-delivered newspapers or magazines, either suspend the subscription or make sure a friend or neighbor will pick up the deliveries.

- If possible and appropriate to your situation, ask a nearby friend or neighbor to park his or her car in your driveway while you're gone.

Drive Danger from Your Door

Would you welcome a burglar, thief, or rapist into your apartment? Stupid question. But many people—unwittingly, of course—do just that. You should not be one of them:

- Never allow a stranger into your home. It's common for intruders to gain entry by playing on your good Samaritan nature. "My car broke down, and I left my cell phone at home. Can I use your phone?" Your answer should be no; however, you may offer to make a phone call for the person: "Is there someone you'd like me to call for you?"

- Unless you are personally acquainted with the person, do not allow a service worker—janitor, repairman, installer—into your apartment without first asking to see his or her identification. You should do this even if you yourself have made the appointment with the person.

- Do not open your door to talk to a stranger. Open the door, and an intruder can push his way right in. Use the peephole, and, awkward though this may be, talk to the stranger through the closed door. If your door does not have a peephole, it should be equipped with a strong chain, so that you can open it slightly to check out identification and talk with the caller.

- Beware of "wrong number" calls in which the caller asks for your number: "Oh. I think I have the wrong number. What number have I reached?" The caller may be trying to connect a name with a number for scam purposes or to identify single females. Do not give out any information to a caller. Just say "You have the wrong number" or ask what number the caller was trying to reach. If the number is not yours, tell the caller he has the wrong number and hang up. If the number he gives is your number, tell the caller that no one by the name he is asking for lives there and hang up.

Cell Phone Savvy

The cell phone made its commercial debut in 1984 in the form of the Motorola Dyna-Tac 8000, known as "the brick" because it was heavy (28 ounces) and big (10 inches high—like a World War II walkie-talkie). It also cost the user a hefty $3,995—not counting connection fees and talk time. Despite all of this, the cellular telephone caught on, so that today there are about 2.5 billion of them in use worldwide.

They can be annoying, of course. Nobody likes listening to one side of a loudmouth conversation conducted in public. And they can be hazardous. Not only are there the obvious dangers of distracted drivers, but people walking and yapping can look pretty mindless and distracted. That is, they look like victims, easy targets.

But cell phone good far outweighs cell phone bad. When you are out and about, always take your cell phone with you. Keep it fully charged. Make sure that you program for speed dial all relevant emergency numbers, especially campus police, as well as the numbers of some reliable friends. If you feel that you are in imminent danger, call 911. Identify yourself, give your location, and explain the problem. Keep walking toward a place of safety, but let the potential assailant *see* that you are talking. Be certain that he sees you make the call. You want the call to look like what it is—purposeful—not idle and oblivious chatter. Look toward him, using your slow glare, the glance that seems to see through the other person but that lets him know that you are very much onto him.

Assess the Threat

How can you tell if someone you see on the street means to hurt you? Unless the person actually attacks, there is no foolproof way to distinguish the dangerous from the harmless. Begin, of course, by trusting your gut. If someone gives you a bad feeling, there is probably a good reason for it, even if you can't put your finger on it. Head for a place of safety. Get ready to use your cell phone to call 911.

Beyond sheer gut instinct, look for these signs:

- A person who does not belong—a stranger on campus or in the neighborhood

- A person with nothing to do—a loiterer

- A person who behaves menacingly or strangely

- A person under unusual stress—in a frantic rush, weaving in and out of other people

- A belligerent or confrontational person who bears down on you, expecting you to get out of the way and probably hoping you won't, so that he can start something

If you can get a look at the person's face, watch for glaring eyes, which look you up and down contemptuously and provocatively. Look for dead eyes, a vacant stare that betrays no emotion but that is plenty creepy. Look for darting eyes, eyes that look wildly this way or that. Look for averted eyes, eyes that glance your way, then look deliberately away to avoid contact. Look for widely dilated pupils, which indicate a person under the influence of a controlled substance.

What should you do when you note any of these body language characteristics? If you are alone, steer clear of the person, seek the company of others, and walk toward someplace safe. Do not run away. Walk purposefully, head up, slowly scanning your surroundings. Do not avoid looking at the person. Let him know, with a glance and a glare, that you are aware of his presence and that you have an idea of what he is up to.

Safe Move

Whenever possible, walk with a friend or friends. Use campus shuttle services, especially after dark. Make it a rule never to walk alone after dark.

Yell, Yell, Yell

If the worst happens, and you are attacked, yell. Yell loudly and keep yelling. Yelling for help is not nearly as effective as yelling directly at the assailant: "No! Get away! No!" Do not stop. Draw attention to yourself. If you can break away, run. But keep yelling.

Responding to a Weapon

If you find yourself facing a person with a gun, knife, or other deadly weapon, you will have to decide whether complying with his demands is your safest course, or whether you should run, or whether you should attempt to disarm the assailant.

Unless you have had professional training in self-defense, the last course is probably too dangerous. If the assailant demands your money or property, it's best to comply. As you do so, look for your chance to get away. Your attacker will be momentarily preoccupied with taking the money, purse, or other item, even if you have put it on the ground. Seize the moment to run. Remember, it's difficult even for highly trained marksmen to hit a moving target, especially one that is moving away from them.

Fight Back

Just about everyone can benefit from taking self-defense classes given by qualified instructors. Check with your campus police department, your physical education department, and student activities, and chances are that you will find a course offered by your school, on campus.

If you are approached or menaced, bring your hands close to your face, palms forward, and yell as loudly and as sharply as possible: "Get back!" This may be sufficient to drive the attacker off.

If you *are* physically attacked—grabbed, choked, punched—your over-riding goal is to force your assailant to break contact so that you can get away.

Breaking Contact

Unless you are well trained in self-defense, punching and kicking are not always effective methods for forcing an attacker to break contact with you. Both moves tend to put you off balance, possibly rendering you even more vulnerable. Your objective should be to get the *attacker* off balance.

If you are grabbed by the wrist, use your free hand to hit the back of the attacker's hand as sharply as possible. Make a fist and drive your knuckles as near as possible to the second and third knuckles of the assailant's hand. Come down hard, as if pounding on a door with your knuckles. Hit hard enough, and the attacker will let go reflexively. When he does, run and yell. *Never turn around to check out the effect of what you've done!* Delay is deadly. You've won a second or two by stunning the attacker. Use that time to put distance between him and you. The farther away you get, the less chance there is that he will renew the attack.

If an attacker goes for your throat, your hair, or even the lapels of your jacket, bury the toe of your foot in his shin. This is not a high kick— trying that will put you off balance—but a low kick aimed upward, scraping and digging into the shin, which is a very sensitive and vulnerable part of the body, with lots and lots of nerve endings. As you do dig into the attacker's shin, if you have a free hand and if at all possible, reach out and grab for the skin under one of the attacker's extended arms. Grab as far up the arm, as close to the armpit, as you can. Twist what you grab. Twist and continue to twist and squeeze while also digging into his shin until he lets go. Typically, he will let go quickly because of reflex. As soon as you feel him break contact, run. Do not look back. Yell and scream through the whole process.

> ### Little Black Book
>
> For guidelines on choosing a self-defense course, take a look at these two websites: Defend University, a research group, offers advice at www.defendu.com/wsdi/ choosing_a_selfdefense_ course.htm, and Wichita State University lists the National Coalition Against Sexual Assault's guidelines at http://webs.wichita.edu/ ?u=police&p=/selfdefense.

Arm Yourself?

Should you carry any weapons for self-defense? The answer is complicated and depends on the laws that apply in your area, the regulations that apply on campus, the degree of training you have in using weapons, your actual willingness to use the weapon, and your physical ability to keep the weapon out of the hands of an attacker.

Although ownership of firearms for protection of one's home or business is widely accepted, obtaining a permit to carry a firearm on your person is a much more difficult process. Using a concealed weapon without a permit—even in self-defense—may carry a mandatory prison sentence. And, of course, virtually no college or university permits students to carry firearms. Finally, the law aside, firearms are very difficult to control, to use effectively, and to use safely unless you are professionally trained and unless you apply your training with regular practice.

If not a gun, what about a knife? Most jurisdictions have laws covering bladed weapons as well as firearms. Local laws typically restrict the type of knife that may be carried, the length of the blade, and so on. Again, probably no college or university permits students to carry knives on campus. It is, of course, possible to carry a small jackknife or box cutter, but, as with firearms, unless you have been thoroughly trained in the use of these as weapons, the chances are great that the implement will be wrested away from you in a fight and used against you or that it will simply prove ineffectual.

Nonlethal weapons such as stun guns and pepper spray or mace are often subject to fewer legal restrictions—although it is your responsibility to find out what laws apply in your area and what rules apply on your campus. Assuming that you can legally use a stun gun in your city or town and on your campus, it's still a weapon that requires training and practice to use properly. If an attacker gets the stun gun away from you, you are at his mercy.

Pepper spray, a chemical spray that burns the eyes (temporarily blinding, disorienting, and disabling an attacker) and mucous membranes, is common. It is subject to at least three major shortcomings, however:

◆ You have to be able to get to it and use it immediately. Your attacker is not going to stand back to give you time to fish it out of your purse.

◆ Like any other weapon, it can be turned against you and be used to disable you. Indeed, many street thugs use pepper spray preemptively to facilitate their attacks.

♦ Pepper spray and mace do not always work on all people. These substances have a limited shelf life, and some people are remarkably resistant to it, especially if they are under the influence of certain drugs.

There is one weapon we all carry and that can be quite effective: a set of keys. They are pointed, serrated, and fit easily in the palm of the hand. If you feel threatened—or as you approach your apartment or your car—take your keys out and insert one between each of your fingers. If you are attacked, start jabbing. Go for the eyes, the throat, and the face. When contact is broken, run. Remember to yell and to keep yelling.

Commit

However you respond to danger—to the possibility of attack or to an actual attack—commit to the response. Focus. Decide to survive. Remember that your goal is to break contact with the attacker and get to a place of safety. This means that you need only temporarily disable or stun the attacker to buy time to get away. Your goal is not to vent your anger, get revenge, or mete out vigilante justice. Your goal is to keep from getting hurt. Your goal is to survive.

The Least You Need to Know

♦ As a human being, you are born with a survival instinct. When your gut tells you that you are in a dangerous place or situation, listen to it and prepare to act.

♦ Assess the security of your environment, and learn to recognize the signs of potential danger in other people.

♦ Be alert to the safety and security of off-campus housing. Take steps to make yourself safe from fire as well as from burglars and other intruders.

♦ If you are menaced or attacked, your overriding goal is to get out of the situation and get away from the potential or actual attacker immediately, while also drawing attention to yourself by yelling.

Emergency!

Here are the key actions to take in common emergency situations.

Accident, Injury, and Medical Emergencies

1. Identify the affected person and make all efforts to aid and comfort that person.

2. Call 911 and provide the following information to the operator:

   ◆ The exact location of the affected person

   ◆ Whether or not the affected person is conscious

   ◆ Whether or not the affected person appears to be breathing

   ◆ Any apparent injuries or medical condition

   ◆ The sex, age, and physical condition of the affected person

3. Call campus security or campus police.

Disasters—Natural and Otherwise

1. Stay calm.

2. Call 911, but since telephone and cell phone circuits often over-load in an emergency, refrain from unnecessary use of the phone and Internet except for critical communications.

3. If a terrorist attack is suspected or confirmed, close windows, turn off air-conditioning units, close doors, and move to interior hallways.

4. Stay on campus and indoors unless instructed otherwise. This is particularly important if the threat is chemical or biological in nature.

5. If instructed to evacuate, follow the directions of trained campus personnel, including public safety officers.

6. If applicable, attempt to stay away from falling debris, glass, heavy equipment, or other objects that may cause damage or injury.

Fire

1. Evacuate the building.

2. Call 911 first, then campus security or campus police. *Make all calls from outside of the building threatened by fire!*

3. Help others account for fellow students, faculty, and others.

4. Do not return to the threatened building to look for unaccounted-for persons or personal belongings, but do advise the responding emergency personnel of any unaccounted-for persons and their possible location.

5. Follow all instructions of campus safety, police, and fire officials.

Lights Out

1. Report any utility disruption to campus safety or campus police. You may have to use a cell phone to do this. In a dormitory, report

to the RA. If no means of reporting the problem are available, calmly leave the building and walk to the campus safety or police office to report the problem.

2. Unless you must leave to report the outage, stay where you are. Campus safety personnel will provide instructions and provide assistance, if needed.

3. If you have access to a flashlight, get it. Use it to assist others.

Violent Threats, Violent Crime

1. Report all violent threats to campus security/campus police.

2. If a suspicious object or package is encountered, do not handle it. Call campus security/campus police immediately.

3. If you witness a crime in progress, call 911 first, then call campus security/campus police.

Shots Fired

1. If you see or hear shots fired, ensure your own safety first. Take cover or, if it is safe to do so, leave the area immediately.

2. If you're in your dorm room, stay there, lock the door, and call 911.

3. Call 911 first, then call campus security/campus police unless the 911 operator instructs you to remain on the phone.

Evacuation Procedures

1. In any obvious emergency, such as fire, leave the threatened building or area immediately but as calmly as possible.

2. Follow all instructions of campus officials.

Index

E

I

S